Villains
Road Crew

Villains Road Crew

A Theatrical Playbook Collection

Albalis Smith
(a.k.a. Lirio Blanco Show)

Copyright © 2025 by Albalis D. Smith

All rights reserved. No part of this book may be reproduced or transmitted in any form or by any means, electronic or mechanical, including photocopying, recording, or any information storage and retrieval system, without permission in writing from the author.

ISBN: 978-1-6653-0800-7 - Paperback
eISBN: 978-1-6653-0801-4 - eBook

These ISBNs are the property of BookLogix for the express purpose of sales and distribution of this title. The content of this book is the property of the copyright holder only. BookLogix does not hold any ownership of the content of this book and is not liable in any way for the materials contained within. The views and opinions expressed in this book are the property of the Author/Copyright holder, and do not necessarily reflect those of BookLogix.

Library of Congress Control Number: 2024922551

∞ This paper meets the requirements of ANSI/NISO Z39.48-1992 (Permanence of Paper)

Cover Painting by Albalis Smith

0 4 1 0 2 5

Dedication

I want to dedicate this book to Billy Ray Smith, my beloved father-in-law. Incidentally, I want to reassure the spirit of my father Guillermo De Jesus Vargas Campos, that he is going to be the recipient of my dedication in the next book I publish. After all, these two men were very good to me while they were alive.

For many years, driving to Paisley, Florida was the highlight of our holidays. That's the city where Billy Ray lived with his sweet wife Nana Kathy. Although he left us in 2017, I always will be very grateful for the kindness and the love he shared with my husband, my daughter, my mother, and I. To honor his memory, I am painting his portrait, which will be on the cover of one of my next books.

Thank you, Bill, for your kindness, humble demeanor, and good sense of humor. You truly have been and will be missed!

— Lirio Blanco Show

Table of Contents

Acknowledgments ix

Introduction xi

Preface xiii

The Plays 1

- The Villains Road Crew 2

- The Business Park 82

Acknowledgments

For many years, my mother's poems have been in the back of my mind. She wrote many poems, mostly in her younger days. When she died, I inherited her belongings. Among them was a bag which contained many papers. When browsing through them, I found her beautiful poems and newspaper clips with the articles she used to write for one of the Panamanian newspapers.

I always knew I had to figure out what to do with my mom's poems. For many years, she asked me what I was planning to do with them. In order to share her writings with the world, I decided to complete my unfinished stories, and published few of them along with two theatrical plays contained in The Moldy Orange Bandage, which was my first book published in the year 2021.

Still, I haven't found a way to share my mom's poems with the world. For a while, I planned to share them in video format, but my husband and I discovered that the movie industry is very saturated. While millions of talented people try to share their wonderful work worldwide, they compete with one another to gain the last soul's attention on earth. After all, humans can't handle so much information contained in all social media platforms. It's impossible.

Without a doubt, I can say, my mom's unpublished poems are my biggest unfinished business. I still don't know if I should scan, print, or type them, to publish an actual book in her honor. Truth be told, if it wasn't for my mom's inspiration, my pen name, Lirio Blanco Show, might have never existed. Strangely enough, I have come to the realization that it is easy to write and publish a book—what isn't easy, is to find the right audience.

If you decided to read book two of The Moldy Orange Bandage, Playbooks and Stories Series, I would like to thank you very much for becoming part of my audience.

Introduction

This is the second in my series of playbooks and stories. While my first book targets the tween and family audience, this second contains two theatrical plays for adults. One of the plays is called *The Villains Road Crew* which I started writing in 2012 in narrative format; it was then called *The Villains Crew*. But it wasn't completed until the year 2021, when I revised it as a theatrical play. For many months, I struggled to find its ultimate title. However, when my husband Mark Smith suggested to incorporate the word "road," I felt in my heart we had arrived upon its final title.

The other play contained in this book is *The Business Park* which I started writing in 2021 and finished in 2022. Without further ado, I welcome you to the second book in my playbook series. We hope you enjoy it!

Preface

The Villains Road Crew and *The Business Park* are two theatrical plays written for adult audiences.

While I write this preface, I am cooking one of my family's favorite dishes; one of the few dishes I can ably prepare. You see, I am not a great cook. While doing so, I started thinking of what to write for the preface of this book. The first thing that came to my mind is *The Villains Road Crew*, which started as a depiction of the average blue-collar worker—those women and men who sweat under the sun while doing vigorous work which shapes our communities.

I don't drive much these days. However, when I do, and glance at a garbage truck driver, a delivery worker, a road worker, or a truck driver, my heart is filled with deep compassion and gratitude for their service to our families and communities. I believe in their hands lie the steering wheel of society's working machine.

While *The Villains Road Crew* is an homage to the blue-collar worker, it exposes one of the greatest weaknesses of humanity throughout history, the tendency of humankind to behave like a herd of sheep. One does and follows what an unknown stranger or government tells one to do.

Personally, I must admit, I do love the supernatural. So, I also added certain supernatural references throughout the play.

As an immigrant from Panama, I also make reference to the homesickness one experiences while living in another land.

The Business Park is an unconscious response to the plot of *The Villains Road Crew*. Of course, I don't want to say much about their plots, but I can tell the audience that both plays are a redemption to the blue-collar worker, and an homage to the deep sentiment foreigners harbor in their hearts; the experiences one faces while living in another country.

Without further delay, I hope you enjoy *The Villains Road Crew* and *The Business Park*. I hope my family and I can see one of these two plays performed on a local stage before I leave this plane.

The Plays

The Villains Road Crew

THE VILLAINS ROAD CREW

Cast:

Joshua Harris
Patrick Razor/Razurlangt
Benign Williams
Tracy Lowery
Nathaniel Davis
Mrs. Adelaide
Carmela Razor/Razurlangt
Nicole Razor
Child 1
Child 2
Child 3
Follower 1
Follower 2
Follower 3
Police officer

(The opening scene consists of two street intersections: The one parallel to the stage is finished, while the one perpendicular to the stage is an unfinished street. The latter is flanked by two parallel sidewalks, one finished and the other un-finished. There is a street sign that points to Clover Street in one direction, and another that points to Sediment Road.
There are two trailers in the background. Each of them has CCTV cameras and a sign that reads: (HARRIS AND COMPANY)

NARRATOR:
On a cloudy afternoon, four workers wearing yellow security vests from the city of Lavender Pond are building a section of new pavement at the intersection of Clover Street and Sediment Road. Joshua Harris is handling the jackhammer machine, while Patrick Razor is picking up the residue and fragments from the rubble. While these two men are performing their duties, Benign Williams and Tracy Lowery are pouring concrete with the pre-formed wooden form which is shaping the new sidewalk. Meanwhile, Nathaniel is standing smoking a cigarette. He is a

very skinny character, who wears a pair of old stained jeans and a T-shirt with a logo which says "Chiller" that can be seen under his security vest.

JOSHUA:
(Yelling at Nathaniel) Hey-yo, Nath! Give me a hand here!

NATHANIEL:
Nah, I'm on my cigarette break, man!
(All men and woman are quietly doing their duties, when another woman passes by the site, and suddenly the men whistle at her. The poor woman hastily leaves the scene to avoid more embarrassment.)

NARRATOR:
All men stop at 10:45 a.m. to take their respective lunch breaks. Joshua is a very quiet worker, while the rest of the crew talks about all topics one can imagine. But that day, they talk about gambling. They were planning to go to a nearby city to test their good fortune. Joshua just stares at the men and nods sideways while chewing the rest of his food.

PATRICK:
(Finishes his food first) Guys! I am

going ahead to keep picking up the rubble.

NARRATOR:
What some of the crew ignored is that Patrick Razor is an unemployed software engineer, who has not found a job in his field, has three children, and is a single parent. His mother currently takes care of his children. He feels some sort of resentment when he hears his coworkers making plans and spending money, while he does not have this luxury. Every piece of solid rock, concrete, or any kind of garbage he disposes of turns into a piece of frustration in his life. One piece of rubble symbolizes his career's frustration; others turn into anger for his marital situation. One wonders why Patrick, who once was a successful software engineer for a worldwide company and traveled around the world with a happy family, ended up alone as a single parent disposing of the city's roadwork waste. Nicole Razor was his wife. After a year of dealing with Patrick's unemployment and the depression caused by the situation itself, she left him. One might ask why a wife would dishonor her man in this

way, but situations and circumstances can change people's minds. The fact is Patrick is now lonely and performing a job he never thought he'd do. What can Patrick do to change this situation? How could he figure out a way to raise his self-esteem? No matter what he does, it seems that all the doors are closed. He has given up any hope or any other way to solve his problems. Of course, he enjoys taking care of his three children, but there is an empty void in his life. He feels like a complete failure. Although he tries to overcome all obstacles, while honoring his job, the emotional emptiness is still there . . . no matter how difficult it is to keep supporting his family. He always wonders, *"What if I try harder?"*

NATHANIEL:
Hey! Yo! Patrick! Do you want to come gamble with us tonight? Me and my buddies always have a sweet time at the pub down yonder.

PATRICK:
I appreciate it Nath, but I cannot. I have to get home and take care of my children and give my mother a break.

(BENIGN WILLIAMS approaches the two talking)

BENIGN:
Man, the more in the pool, the better! Come on! My wife can take care of your kiddos tonight! Come with us!

NATHANIEL:
I can even pick you up myself!

PATRICK:
Guys, I appreciate it, but I cannot. I don't have money to gamble.

NATHANIEL:
Phew! That's not a problem, my man! I can lend you a good sum, and you can make four times the amount. I won't charge you interest. Let's say it's just one big I. O. U. (He laughs)

JOSHUA:
Hey, guys! Leave Patrick alone. If he does not want to come tonight, don't pressure him into it.

BENIGN:
I am actually sensing our good friend here is about to make up his mind and come with us tonight! (He laughs) Aren't you, Patrick? Huh?

(PATRICK smiles over the awkwardness of the conversation)

JOSHUA:
Bennie, Bennie, Bennie. Leave the bro alone, man!

NATHANIEL:
My Pat! My Pat! My man! Sometimes I can pay my rent with the money I make in the games. It's mucha mula man! Much, much, much!

PATRICK:
Mucha mula? What is that?

JOSHUA:
(Irritated) Guys! Go! Go back to work right now!

(All men restart their duties. TRACY approaches PATRICK while he still is picking up the rubble)

TRACY:
Patrick! Why are you here? How is your job search? This is not the place for you, here! You know that, right?

PATRICK:
Oh Tracy, don't start with the same sermon again! I know exactly what I am doing!

TRACY:
Oh really? And what is that? You know what I heard, Patrick? You know what I heard?

PATRICK:
I don't want to hear your American women gossips, Tracy. I love you, you are

my best pal—but don't get me started, please!

TRACY:
Patrick, when I brought you here six months ago, I did it out of the sense of urgency for your situation, if you know what I mean. You need to move on, Patrick, you still owe all that pointless college tuition. And I am going to tell you what I heard; your mother cannot deal with the three kids! Did you hear me?

PATRICK:
What are you talking about, Tracy? Besides, she is here temporarily. Her visa only lasts six months. She has to go back to her country soon.

TRACY:
I don't know about visa or any of those immigration terms. The only thing I can tell you is that my Aunt Elizabeth . . . You know, the one with the twisted cane?

PATRICK:
Yes, Tracy, I know the one with the glass eye and cane!

TRACY:
Exactly! Her!

PATRICK:
What about her, Tracy?

TRACY:
She told me! You know, my Aunt Elizabeth!

PATRICK:
Yes, yes! Your aunt! Please continue, Tracy!

TRACY:
She saw your mom at the grocery store, crying, while your youngest kid was running loops around the store. I don't know if you know, Pat, but your mom fell that day on the floor of that store and sprained her ankle.

PATRICK:
What? I haven't heard about any of this!

TRACY:
You haven't noticed her limping?

PATRICK:
Tracy, how many hours a week do we work here? Twelve hours! Sometimes more! I go straight home, eat, say goodnight to the kids and my mom and go to bed.

TRACY:
That is you, Pat. I just work my eight hours and go home. If I don't cook, we don't eat, so I am out of here right

on the dot. But Pat, there's no excuse for you not knowing that your mother is hurt.

PATRICK:
Oh, boy! What am I going to do? She is not insured in this country! I cannot pay childcare! I can't-

(TRACY stops him abruptly)

TRACY:
Pat!

JOSHUA:
What the heck do you think you two you are doing? Don't test me. Tracy! Please, go back to your work!

TRACY:
Joshua, did you hear about his mother falling at the grocery store?

JOSHUA:
Tracy, that's enough! Go back to work! And you, Patrick, what is this deal I hear of your mom falling at the store?

PATRICK:
(Continues working while talking) Tracy just told me. It appears she heard this from a third party.

JOSHUA:
Does your mom live with you?

PATRICK:
Yes, sort of. She came to the US to help me with my kids.

JOSHUA:
How old is your mother?

PATRICK:
She is in her mid-seventies.

JOSHUA:
Man, she is kind of old to be babysitting for you! WOW!

PATRICK:
If you don't mind, I prefer not to talk about my private matters anymore.

JOSHUA:
Okay. No problem!
(NATHANIEL and BENIGN approach the two men)

NATHANIEL:
A little gambling won't hurt, Patrick!

BENIGN:
Yeah, man! It's your call.

PATRICK:
I already said what I have to say. (He resumes working)

(TRACY approaches the scene, as well as MRS. ADELAIDE. MRS. ADELAIDE is pushing a little cart which carries two big, rectangular coolers and a big pot of coffee.)

TRACY:
Hey, guys! Mrs. Adelaide is here!
(Gathers around MRS. ADELAIDE)

MRS. ADELAIDE:
Hey everyone! Fresh crepes, hot coffee and sweet Mrs. Adelaide have arrived!
(She starts unfolding a couple of foldable chairs.)

NATHANIEL:
Mrs. Adelaide! It's about time!

MRS. ADELAIDE:
Babe, you know I cannot miss my boys!

BENIGN:
Come on, Mrs. Adelaide! Let me give you a big, big hug! Come on!

MRS. ADELAIDE:
Come on, babe! (Both hug)

(PATRICK approaches JOSHUA HARRIS.)

PATRICK:
Who is this person that just arrived?

JOSHUA:
You haven't met Mrs. Adelaide?

PATRICK:
No.

JOSHUA:
She comes every now and then, selling her crepes from her mobile cart. We love her, man!

PATRICK:
Are you sure she just sells crepes? I heard there are tons of street food vendors who sell other things, if you know what I mean!

JOSHUA:
Come on, man! You can't just see bad things everywhere!

MRS. ADELAIDE:
Come on girls and boys, sit and enjoy!

JOSHUA:
Mrs. Adelaide, give me two crepes with scrambled eggs and a fresh cup of that coffee of yours!

MRS. ADELAIDE:
Sounds good, Joshua. Come on! (Both characters hug)

JOSHUA:
Why haven't I seen you in here for a while, Mrs. Adelaide?

(MRS. ADELAIDE opens the cooler, takes out a dish—a crepe and a little container—and starts serving the crepe and the egg on the dish)

MRS. ADELAIDE:
Oh, Joshie! Don't let me bore you with my silly stories. I am here today and that's what matters, no? Here! Two crepes with scrambled eggs! (Slowly pours coffee in a big mug) Mrs. Adelaide's great coffee here! (She laughs)

JOSHUA:
Thank you, Ma'am! I have longed for your crepes and coffee for weeks!

MRS. ADELAIDE:
Well, here we are!

TRACY:
Mrs. Adelaide!

MRS. ADELAIDE:
Oh, my dear Tracy! Come on here! (Both women hug while PATRICK approaches them)

TRACY:
Patrick! Mrs. Adelaide's food is the best! Come! Sit in the chair. (Pointing at a foldable chair)

PATRICK:
No, Tracy! I have to work!

TRACY:
Pat, what the heck! Joshua is our boss, and he is enjoying himself!

PATRICK:
Well, Tracy, that's him! It's his business—not mine!

TRACY:
Come on Pat, take a break! Have fun! Come on! (Pulls one of PATRICK'S arms)

PATRICK:
Tracy, leave me alone! That is why you—a woman of your age is here, working under the sun, doing meaningless tasks, and covered in dust and dirt!

TRACY:
What is that supposed to mean, Patrick Razor? How freaking dare you? You of all people! How dare you talk to me like that?

PATRICK:
That is why this country is as it is now! People just want to do the minimum and expect great results!

TRACY:
You shut your mouth right now, Patrick Razor! How dare you! If I am here, it's because of my own business. I have driven eighteen-wheelers, bulldozers, cranes, transit buses, and I have raised five children! And do you know why I am here, Patrick Razor? I am here because

I want to be here. I am here because I love sweating under the sun, building things with my hands. It fulfills me to know that one day, one of my kids is going to walk over one of the streets I helped to build, or enter a building where I nailed a piece of sheetrock, or simply—

(PATRICK interrupts her)

PATRICK:
But where all those jobs have brought you, Tracy? Where? Working among ex-convicts? Do you think I don't know the truth? I know well that Nathaniel, Benign, and even Joshua are criminals! With all those tattoos covering their bodies—their gambling, the drinking, and who knows what else.

TRACY:
Yes, Patrick. They have robbed, and have done very bad things, but they are trying to live a good life now. The bad instinct is like that of a wild animal; we never know when it will wake up. And let me tell you something else, thanks to the *ex-convict* Joshua, I have been able to pay the tuition for most of my kids. You know very well my husband does not make a lot of money. I want to be

under the sun so that they don't have to be! Yes, I know these guys have done bad deeds, but tell me Patrick, what is the difference between any of them and your former co-worker who stole your software program at your previous job? Isn't he now the director of development? Did he not steal? Huh? Or the other one that threw you under the bus with your supervisor and got you fired—losing your entire retirement fund? Can't that be considered as conspiracy and treason? Not to mention the other reason you lost your job was because you're a foreigner. They robbed you of the way to make your living! Do you want me to keep going with the list?

PATRICK:
So you're trying to tell me I should have remained at a job with coworkers who had so thoroughly betrayed me?

TRACY:
Perhaps.

PATRICK:
(Aghast) Are you out of your—

MRS. ADELAIDE:
Kids! What is happening here?

TRACY:
Excuse me, Mrs. Adelaide, but I need to walk away for a few minutes.

MRS. ADELAIDE:
That's fine, child! Go ahead! And you! (Approaching PATRICK) what's your name again?

PATRICK:
Patrick.

MRS. ADELAIDE:
Patrick. I am Mrs. Adelaide, nice to meet you! Come and join us! I have enough warm food for an entire troop! Come!

PATRICK:
I don't want to be rude, but I have to work.

(MRS. ADELAIDE pulls him by the arm)

MRS. ADELAIDE:
Come and sit!

PATRICK:
But . . .

MRS. ADELAIDE:
No buts! Sit and enjoy my food, it's on the house! (PATRICK sits, reluctantly)

MRS. ADELAIDE:
Here! I have crepes with scrambled eggs

and sausage, which one would you like to try?

PATRICK:
(Hesitates) Sausage.

MRS. ADELAIDE:
Good choice! You know, Patrick, I made the crepes from scratch and I grow all the herbs and vegetables that I use for my cooking.

(PATRICK appears to be clueless.)

PATRICK:
Excuse me, Ma'am, I really don't want to be rude, but I don't really follow what you are trying to say!

JOSHUA:
Patrick! Don't you dare to be condescending to Mrs. Adelaide, that kind of stuff just infuriates me!

(PATRICK abruptly stands, gives the food to JOSHUA and leaves to keep working.)

JOSHUA:
Here, Mrs. Adelaide (gives the food to her) I don't know what is going on with him today, he usually is very calm and quiet.

(MRS. ADELAIDE quietly follows PATRICK with her eyes. TRACY approaches the scene)

TRACY:
I don't know why I brought him here!
This is going to ruin our very long
friendship!

JOSHUA:
I only hired the guy cause you asked me
to, Tracy. Why are you whining now? Now
the guy is causing trouble here.

TRACY:
Joshua, the guy is going through a very
rough patch.

JOSHUA:
So? That ain't my problem, Tracy!

MRS. ADELAIDE:
That kid does not belong here. What is
he doing here?

TRACY:
I met him when I was a driver for the
city transit authority. We were very
young, and he always had a big smile
in his face when got on the bus. Since
then, I don't know why, but we became
very good friends.

MRS. ADELAIDE:
How long ago?

TRACY:
Twenty-something years . . .

MRS. ADELAIDE:
He does not seem to be cut for this kind of job. Something about him . . . There is something obscure about him, Tracy!

TRACY:
Obscure? You mean dark?

MRS. ADELAIDE:
Yes, Tracy, something dark.

JOSHUA:
Mrs. Adelaide and Tracy, leave your hocus pocus out of this and let's keep working!

MRS. ADELAIDE:
Joshie, do you mind if I stay a little longer on your site today?

JOSHUA:
You can stay all day if you want, Mrs. Adelaide. But don't take time from my crew! Why do you want to stay, anyway?

MRS. ADELAIDE:
I want to observe something.

JOSHUA:
That Razor fellow! You are too old for that sort of thing! (He laughs)

MRS. ADELAIDE:
Oh, Joshie! Don't be absurd! By the way, I hear some sort of accent there!

JOSHUA:
You got it! He is from Europe. In fact, his last name is not Razor. It's Razurlangt.

MRS. ADELAIDE:
Why did he change it?

JOSHUA:
No one could pronounce the darn last name, so he made it shorter. But still, I don't understand why you are so interested in him!

MRS. ADELAIDE:
Joshie, that boy is in serious trouble. Tell me, has he lost his family, or let's say a job recently?

JOSHUA:
Mrs. Adelaide, how did you know?

MRS. ADELAIDE:
Know what?

JOSHUA:
His wife left him and his kids recently. He hasn't been able to keep a job and he's lost all of his money before he started working here.

MRS. ADELAIDE:
Joshie, listen to me! That boy is going to keep losing everything! Jobs, relationships, and possibly his own life!

JOSHUA:
Lord have mercy! What the heck are you talking about, Mrs. Adelaide?

MRS. ADELAIDE:
Joshie, this boy is under a spell!

JOSHUA:
Spell? What the heck, Mrs. Adelaide? You know I don't believe in any of that—that's soap opera material.

MRS. ADELAIDE:
Yes! Spells and witchcraft, Joshie! The blackest of black magic!

JOSHUA:
What the heck! Can he pass any of that bad stuff to any of us?

MRS. ADELAIDE:
Oh, no! Joshie, the hex that poor boy has on him? It holds only his name. But primarily, his last name.

JOSHUA:
But what can he do?

MRS. ADELAIDE:
Nothing!

JOSHUA:
Nothing? Lord have mercy!

MRS. ADELAIDE:
That's right! Nothing! It's the

trickiest part of it all. He has to figure out what to do by himself.

JOSHUA:
Well, Mrs. Adelaide, what can I do to help the poor guy out?

MRS. ADELAIDE:
You? Absolutely nothing! But Joshie, you can pray for him when you are alone! Just tell God: "Lord! Cover this fellow, Patrick Razor, blah, blah—whatever the rest of his last name is—with your light." That's it!

JOSHUA:
But he should know he has some bad juju going on!

MRS. ADELAIDE:
Nah, Joshie! Let it be! Well, I am leaving now. But Joshie, this boy is going to need lots of prayers! Bad things are going to keep happening to him! I'll come back later—that's for sure!

JOSHUA:
Mrs. Adelaide, how come you know about this juju stuff?

MRS. ADELAIDE:
Boy, I know my own tale! That's all I can say! You take care now, please!

(BOTH hug. MRS. ADELAIDE leaves the scene while BENIGN approaches JOSHUA)

BENIGN:
What was that all about?

JOSHUA:
Nothing, Benign. You know Mrs. Adelaide. She always wants to help all people (He laughs) Let's get to work!

(JOSHUA stays silent for few seconds, starts massaging his chin with his left hand's index finger. TRACY approaches the scene)

TRACY:
What's up, Joshua? What did Mrs. Adelaide tell you?

JOSHUA:
Nah, I am a guy. I don't repeat stuff.

TRACY:
Joshua! Now I am scared! If you don't want to tell me, it must be bad.

JOSHUA:
You know this Razor guy pretty well, huh? (TRACY nods) And he is a good guy? (She nods again) What do you know about him from his time in Europe? He had to be a kid then!

TRACY:
Oh boy, Joshua. Don't ask me that!

JOSHUA:
Why?

TRACY:
I can't. I really can't.

JOSHUA:
What country in Europe did he grow up in?

TRACY:
Somewhere north—near Norway—I don't really know. He never talks about that. Look Joshua, you are not going to find a harder working man than him.

JOSHUA:
Finland? North Europe? What the heck? No one leaves any of those countries anymore to move to The US in these modern days! Those countries are in the top ten best countries in the world. What the freak?

TRACY:
Josh, I don't know what Mrs. Adelaide told you, and I might argue with Patrick from time to time, but I am not going to allow you to bring his name down.

JOSHUA:
Wait! That is not my intention, trust me! I just don't understand what a software developer is doing here, under the

sun, clearing up sites. You have to grant my right to be concerned—and this is my business, you know!

TRACY:
What are you concerned about now?

JOSHUA:
It's been six months since I hired him. Don't you think it's about time for him to go and find something related to his line of work?

TRACY:
Do you want to fire him, Joshua? You are going to get in serious trouble with me if you do!

JOSHUA:
I don't want to fire anyone! And furthermore, don't forget who the boss is here, Tracy.

TRACY:
Are you going to bring your macho card here, Joshua? The male power, huh? And on top of that, the ethnic card. Why all those questions regarding Patrick's country of origin? What did Mrs. Adelaide tell you? Tell me now!

JOSHUA:
That *he* is a victim of a spell—so there!

TRACY:
(Lower her eyesight to the floors) Oh, that . . .

JOSHUA:
Oh, that? You knew?

TRACY:
The question is how Mrs. Adelaide knew. That is completely impossible!

JOSHUA:
I don't know how, Tracy. What I want to be sure and certain about is that his bad juju is not contagious!

TRACY:
Joshua, don't worry! That is sadly Patrick's own thing, and no, it's not contagious.

JOSHUA:
What do you know about this? Now I do have to know!

TRACY:
It's the reason he moved to the US. That job was done over there, on the other side of the ocean, in the old continent.

JOSHUA:
You are telling me this thing has been with him for more than twenty years?

TRACY:
Oh, man! Even longer! I used to take him

to witch doctors down in Miami to try to help him, but the job is not of African origin. It's European magic—very different from what you find in the Caribbean.

JOSHUA:
So, is there a cure?

TRACY:
Yes, I imagine so! But it would require him to go back to Europe and deal with it, and he does not want to do that. It might cost him his life. That's why he is working this job.

JOSHUA:
What the heck?

TRACY:
He feels better under the sun. Sweating helps him. Do you understand? Back then, being a software engineer required him to be indoors and seated most of the time. Here he feels rejuvenated!

JOSHUA:
You got to be kidding me, Tracy. I hate this heat! I am so freaking tired of sweating.

TRACY:
Then why are you still working in physical labor?

JOSHUA:
Because I build stuff. You know that better than anyone, Tracy!

TRACY:
Then let Patrick be! Let him sweat, feel nature, and receive the sunlight, which is the only thing he can do.

JOSHUA:
Why? Does the sun cure bad juju?

TRACY:
I don't know about that, but it doesn't hurt either!

(TRACY and JOSHUA start laughing and teasing each other. Suddenly, from the left, a woman enters the scene. It is PATRICK'S wife NICOLE RAZOR. TRACY becomes angry as she notices NICOLE.)

TRACY:
What the freak of the freakiest freaky freaks are you doing here?

NICOLE:
That is none of your business. Do me a favor and go fetch my husband!

TRACY:
Husband? (She laughs) Don't make me laugh!

JOSHUA:
(Looking to NICOLE, he shows her a piece of paper) Ma'am, do you see this paper?

NICOLE:
Yes! I am not blind, you know!

JOSHUA:
This happens to be my liability insurance certificate. I have a limit of people that can be on my site, ma'am! And if something happens to you, I will get in serious trouble, which I am not willing to go through for you! So, get the heck off of my site!

NICOLE:
Who do you think you are?

JOSHUA:
Not your husband, that's for sure. Thank God.

TRACY:
Amen to that, Josh! You don't know who this woman is and what she is capable of!

NICOLE:
You said it yourself, Tracy. So, go now and fetch my husband.

(BENIGN and NATHANIEL approach the scene)

NATHANIEL:
Ma'am, you heard the boss-man, here. Leave our site now!

NICOLE:
(Takes her phone out of her purse) I am going to record you all with my phone, and the entire planet will see the viral video of you mistreating and harassing a defenseless woman!

JOSHUA:
Too late, ma'am! I pay for 24/7 CCTV service, just look at my trailers! (Nicole glances the cameras) Do you think you are the first wife that has come to threaten my site? No ma'am, you are not!

NICOLE:
(Points her cell phone to the crowd and talks to JOSHUA) Who is your boss? Give me your boss' phone number. I'm going to file a complaint about how you are treating me! Give it to me now, or I will send this video. I am a social influencer, you know. I want the number, I want the number now. I want the number, and I want the number, now, now, now! I want the number right now!

(NICOLE continues to insist for the number as PATRICK approaches)

PATRICK:
(Completely flabbergasted) What are you doing here, Nicole? Are you trying to get me fired?

(ALL in the scene flank both sides of PATRICK)

NICOLE:
Do you think you and your thugs here are going to intimidate me? (She paces side to side, still filming with her cell phone) Everybody is watching this right now! (She laughs)

PATRICK:
Then *everybody* will pay you from their own salary, because if I get fired today, you won't have money to eat tomorrow.

NICOLE:
What an idiot, you are! I have patrons in my channel. I can destroy you and your thugs with this video right now. My followers do what I want them to do. I no longer need your sad allowance! Boo hoo!

(MRS. ADELAIDE makes her entrance. She calmly pushes her food cart, and runs it over NICOLE'S feet)

NICOLE:
Ay! Ay! This witch is trying to kill me!

MRS. ADELAIDE:
Oh, hush your mouth. Let me ask you, did my cart run over the rest of the gang's feet?

NICOLE:
No. Just mine, you old bat!

MRS. ADELAIDE:
Well, that's because those other feet are standing in the place where they belong and yours ma'am, don't belong on this site! So leave now!

NICOLE:
But . . .

MRS. ADELAIDE:
(With tremendous authority) NO BUTS, MA'AM! LEAVE NOW!

ALL: Leave now!

NICOLE:
Patrick, this is not going to end like this! You will hear from me when I get home!

PATRICK:
Home? The home you abandoned six months ago? The home where you left your three children? The home where you have not cooked a meal, nor cleaned since you left us? That place is not your home anymore, and don't even pretend you have the right to call it home. Because people like you don't have homes. People like you have musty caves, as gloomy and dark as your own souls! Now get out of here!

TRACY:
Oh no, Pat! No, no, no! Let's be quiet. All hush right now! (She glances side to side) We need to be on the lookout for her patron-followers! Does anyone see any of them? So willing to come and risk their own necks for this so-called social influencer! (She laughs)

(EVERYONE glances left and right and sees no one else is approaching)

NICOLE:
Patrick! You will hear from me. This does not end here.

PATRICK:
I will be waiting! Just set the time, and I will be waiting for you and your followers!

MRS. ADELAIDE:
And this time ma'am, he won't be alone! (MRS. ADELAIDE and NICOLE exchange dramatic glances. NICOLE exits the scene hastily. All lights dim down)

Intermission

(The scene takes place in a small, dark apartment with a window facing the street. There are two armchairs, a dining table with four chairs around it, and a credenza with a vase and a punch bowl that appears to be expensive. PATRICK RAZOR'S mother CARMELA RAZOR, is seated in one of the armchairs reading to two of her grandkids. Both children are close to falling sleep. She appears to be exhausted and slowly falls asleep as well. Patrick opens the door and carefully closes it. He very gently takes the younger of the two children, and carries him to the other room. His mother awakens, then guides the oldest away to his room. After a few seconds, PATRICK comes back and hugs his mother and starts sobbing.)

PATRICK:
Mom! (Sobs) Please, forgive me!

CARMELA:
Perdogive quet? (Language from the Republic of Pariahcalais)
Forgive what?

PATRICK:
Perdogive mei, suur piet!
Forgive me, your foot!

CARMELA:
Quet pasans conth mie piet?
What has happened with my foot?

PATRICK:
Oh mather! Yoi sew, yoi sew!
Oh mother! I know, I know!

(There is a knock on the door. PATRICK approaches the door and opens it.)

TRACY:
Patrick, I came to see how you guys are doing after all that mess that your so-called wife caused at work.

PATRICK:
You did not have to come all the way here, Tracy, but I appreciate it!

CARMELA:
Tracy, dear! (TRACY walks toward CARMELA, who is still sitting in the armchair, and both women hug) It's so good to see you! But what happened with Nicole, something at work, you said?

PATRICK:
Mother, it's nothing. Please, don't worry! Why don't we talk about something else, Tracy, huh?

TRACY:
Oh, yes, of course—something else! By

the way, Mrs. Razurlangt, where is it that you guys are from?

CARMELA:
We are from Pariahcalais Island, a very small island in the north of Europe.

TRACY:
Pariah . . . Parilican . . . Pelican Island? Are there a lot of pelicans there?

PATRICK:
How so?

TRACY:
Sounds like pelican to me!

(Patrick and Carmela laugh)

PATRICK:
Pariahcalais! Not pelican! You made me laugh. Sometimes we have pelicans as well! (She laughs)

TRACY:
Pariahcalais Island? I never heard of that place.

CARMELA:
There is nothing to know about my country. We do not have much money and we don't produce a lot of exported items.

TRACY:
So, what is your country's major source of income, then?

CARMELA:
I guess entertainment-tourism. And fish! Yes, fish.

TRACY:
Still, I have never heard of your island.

PATRICK:
Our country is not like any other, Tracy. Our entire infrastructure is controlled and managed by the big, Nordic countries.

TRACY:
You mean Finland, Denmark or Norway?

PATRICK:
Something like that. We just pay our taxes, which cover our services and their services.

TRACY:
So, Patrick, if your country does not produce anything, what do you eat then?

CARMELA:
We have a mandatory agricultural program for the youth with ages ranging from eighteen to twenty-three. The US has military, and other countries have mandatory military service as well. *We* have agricultural service.

TRACY:
What the heck is that? Agricultural service?

CARMELA:
Yes. And many people enjoy the agricultural service so much that after they retire, they often continue to help with it. They enjoy spending time with the young people and perks of the service. You see, there are horticultural gardens in each community. And each of them have facilities that include restrooms, showers, sleeping accommodations, and even saunas.

TRACY:
Oh boy, Carmela, that sounds like communism! Oh, boy! No wonder Patrick left that place!

CARMELA:
Oh, no, Tracy. For us, it is independence. We do not pay for any fruit or vegetables we consume in our country. Each of them is given to us by nature. Therefore, it is illegal to buy or sell produce.

TRACY:
What the heck?

PATRICK:
Again, we directly pay the government a special tax that covers the support of the people that participate in the agricultural program. They don't have to pay for rent or anything, and after they finish with their two years of service, most of them go to college, which is also paid with our taxes.

TRACY:
Guys, if you are not allowed to sell any produce, how can people make money in your country? That is nuts!

PATRICK:
You can buy or sell human actions, not God's. God cannot cook meals for the people, can He? There are tons of people that own restaurants, Tracy. They charge only for the labor involved, not for the actual food items. The same applies to milk, eggs and cheese. When the farmers sell those items, they just charge for the labor that it took to acquire them.

TRACY:
What about meat? Do you even eat meat?

CARMELA:
People eat meat just to survive. It is illegal to eat meat just for the fun of it. Animals are given to us by God.

Therefore, we cannot pay God for giving animals to us, so we do not eat living creatures—with the exception of people who live in the woods and hunt to survive.

TRACY:
Oh, boy! Oh, boy! So you guys are vegan? That is just crazy.

PATRICK:
No, we are not vegan. We just do not eat animals unless it is a matter of survival. Most of the people that live in rural areas actually hunt during hunting season, and store their meat for the winter.

TRACY:
Patrick, I am so sorry. I did not know any of this.

PATRICK:
Hey, Tracy, when I left Pariahcalais, I did it to never return. You will not see me following any of those traditions here, in the US.

TRACY:
What about you, Carmela?

CARMELA:
Tracy, I am an old woman. I still live there. I am here because my son needs

help, but I love my country with all my heart. It is beautiful to me!

TRACY:
So, are you waiting to go back to Pelican Island to check your leg?

CARMELA:
Of course. I cannot go to the doctor here in your country. I have made appointments with a few of them, but no one wants to see me because I do not have insurance, and I am an old woman. I didn't tell Patrick about my leg for that reason. There was no point for me to tell him because I cannot even be checked. When I heard about the insurance, I did not know what they were talking about. In Pariahcalais, there is no health insurance, and everyone can be seen in the health system program.

TRACY:
Don't tell me, Carmela. Is it also free? (She laughs)

CARMELA:
Well, no, Tracy. We pay taxes for that as well. Our healthcare workers go to each community from time to time, providing medical checkups, vaccinations and they even help to control the birth rate—providing counseling and birth

control methods to those who are not attending any sort of school. Because we do not eat tons of meat, diabetes and cancer are almost nonexistent.

TRACY:
So, not many people go to the doctors?

CARMELA:
Not really . . . except us, the elderly population.

TRACY:
In other words, your country is peachy!

PATRICK:
Tracy, please don't be cynical. This is the exact reason for why, in all these years, I've never spoken about my country. Our country is ideal in many ways, but many young people leave as soon as they can.

TRACY:
I don't blame them. Who wants to spend two years picking up vegetables, for God's sake?

PATRICK:
We both did it, Tracy. That's the reason I enjoy working with you at the site so much. It reminds me of those days.

TRACY:
Ah, I see. Wait a minute! What about the spell?

CARMELA:
That is another reason people leave my country. A good number of the population solves everything with magic there. Our country is made with all the tribes that never belonged on the continent—the outcasts and the misfits. Many kept the bad influence of the magic practiced for centuries in Central Europe.

TRACY:
Carmela, I have tried to help your son, but it is impossible. The juju they practice here in the bayou or Florida is not the same as your country. What exactly happened?

(Knock on door)

PATRICK:
Who's there?

NATHANIEL:
It's me, Nathaniel.

PATRICK:
(Referring to TRACY) What is he doing here? (Opens the door) Nathaniel! What are you doing here?

NATHANIEL:
I got here as soon as I could! (Sounds exhausted) Joshua's trailers have been burned down completely!

PATRICK:
What? How?

NATHANIEL:
Man, your wife's followers came after we left the site and burned the trailers. They spray painted obscenities on the sidewalk and the street we built. But that isn't all!

PATRICK:
Talk man, talk!

NATHANIEL:
While they were vandalizing, Joshua was still there and he got hurt by one of those guys.

TRACY:
(Emotionally) Where is Joshua?

NATHANIEL:
Benign rode with him in the ambulance toward the hospital.

TRACY:
I have to go, now!

NATHANIEL:
Don't even think about it, Tracy!

PATRICK:
Why can't Tracy go to see Joshua?

NATHANIEL:
I saw those people coming in this direction, man!

PATRICK:
What are you talking about? Why here?

NATHANIEL:
I don't know, man! I really don't know!

CARMELA:
Patrick, what are you going to do?

PATRICK:
Well! Call the police!

NATHANIEL:
Man, I've got to go! I can't be here when the cops come!

PATRICK:
What?

TRACY:
Yes, he has some issues with his parole. Go Nath! Go right now!

NATHANIEL:
Yes ma'am, I am heading to the hospital.

PATRICK:
Hey, Nath! Thanks for coming.

NATHANIEL:
Hey, man, don't mention it! (Leaves the scene)

TRACY:
Oh, Lord! Joshua is like a father to me. I need to call Benign . . . (She takes her phone and dials his number)

(PATRICK and CARMELA hold hands as they stare at TRACY)

TRACY:
Benign! How is Joshie? (Listens) Huh? Ah . . . Huh? What? Okay! (Hangs up the phone)

PATRICK:
Talk!

TRACY:
He was shot, Patrick! (She starts crying desperately) What the heck is going on? Joshua spent ten years in jail. He has had his business for twenty years and was never shot! (Cries more)

PATRICK:
Tracy, I think this is my fault. If it was not for my ex-wife, none of those people would be doing this!

TRACY:
Why are they doing this? What does she want from you? She left you, didn't she?

PATRICK:
She is the most selfish woman I have ever met. I have no idea what she wants!

(Someone knocks on the door.)

TRACY:
Oh no! Don't open it, Patrick! It must be the followers!

PATRICK:
Who is this?

MRS. ADELAIDE:
It's me, Mrs. Adelaide!

TRACY:
Open! Open the door!

(PATRICK opens the door)

TRACY:
Mrs. Adelaide! (Both women hug and cry) What are you doing here?

MRS. ADELAIDE:
I heard about what happened to Joshie, and I knew that this gentleman (points to PATRICK) was the next in the list.

PATRICK:
How do you know?

CARMELA:
I know how she knows!

(CARMELA and MRS. ADELAIDE exchange deep glances.)

TRACY:
Do you know each other or something? (Both women keep looking straight to each other's eyes.)

MRS. ADELAIDE:
No. But I can feel her voice, the deepest voice of her being.

(Both women hold hands for a few seconds.)

CARMELA:
Your name is Mrs. Adelaide?

MRS. ADELAIDE:
Exactly!

CARMELA:
I am Carmela Razurlangt, Patrick's mother.

MRS. ADELAIDE:
Nice to meet you, Carmela.

CARMELA:
I believe you and I know what this is about, don't you?

MRS. ADELAIDE:
Yes.

PATRICK:
What do you two mean?

CARMELA:
This has to do with Pariahcalais son!

MRS. ADELAIDE:
Yes, your country!

(Noises come from the street. All of a sudden, a rock is thrown through the window and no one is hurt. PATRICK'S cell phone rings.)

PATRICK:
Hello! (Everyone becomes silent for a few seconds) Have you gone mad? Why are you doing this? Your three children live here—did you forget that already? What is it exactly that you want, Nicole? (Listens) Oh, now you want them? You abandoned them six months ago! I am never going to give up my children! Did you hear me? Wait! What? Are you high?

MRS. ADELAIDE:
Tracy, please go and stay with the kids.

TRACY:
Why? I think Carmela can stay with them.

MRS. ADELAIDE:
(Emphatically) No. Carmela stays here with me!

CARMELA:
Yes, I'll stay here.

(TRACY reluctantly agrees and leaves the scene. The noises from outside become louder before they suddenly hear gunshots.)

PATRICK:
Mather! I'll call the police. (He dials the number in his phone) Hello, Police? This is Patrick Razor, from 15 Divinity Street! Yes! Yes, sir! It's me! Did you? Oh, good! We will be waiting. Thank you.

CARMELA:
What happened, son?

PATRICK:
Someone called the police earlier. They're on their way!

(CARMELA and MRS. ADELAIDE hold hands in prayer. Someone tries to open the door while knocking)

NICOLE:
(From outside) Open the door, Patrick! Open it now, I tell you!

PATRICK:
No! You don't have any right to come inside!

NICOLE:
Ah, no? We will see about that!

(People start kicking the door and successfully break it and enter the apartment. NICOLE and her followers hold out their phones, pointing them toward PATRICK to film him.)

PATRICK:
What are you doing here?

NICOLE:
I came to take my kids!

PATRICK:
Tell these people to leave now!

NICOLE:
No! No! No!

(The followers start saying "no" as well)

PATRICK:
This is between us! We don't have to vent our private life with these strangers!

FOLLOWER 1:
It's not private! We are here for Nicole. Get out of the way! We are going to get her children out of this apartment!

PATRICK:
Are you crazy? Do you want to be charged with kidnapping and home invasion?

NICOLE:
No one is going to be charged with anything. They are my children!

CARMELA:
You left them, Nicole! How are you going to support them without working?

NICOLE:
Oh, don't you worry, old woman! Your son will be required to provide me child support and an allowance to cover my care.

PATRICK:
Oh, yeah? How am I supposed to support you? Have you forgotten that you and your people here destroyed my workplace today?

NICOLE:
That is not my problem! Not my problem! Not my problem!

FOLLOWER 2:
We all are going to support her!

(All followers chant, "Yes! Yes! Yes!")

FOLLOWER 1:
We are her patrons!

(MRS. ADELAIDE walks and everybody moves away, as if an invisible power forces them to walk backward.)

MRS. ADELAIDE:
Patrons? Okay. Tell me, why are you her patron? What merits or skills does she have?

FOLLOWER 2:
She is a victim. Through her channel, she tells us daily of all she has lived through and she has inspired us. She is not alone anymore!

CARMELA:
Victim of what, for God's sake?

NICOLE:
I am a victim of your son, Carmela!

CARMELA:
He is the victim, you American woman! What happened to you? You were not like this when I met you. You were quiet, sweet and dedicated to making your home a warm and welcoming place. What happened to you?

MRS. ADELAIDE:
Carmela, I think you and I know what happened!

CARMELA:
(Sobs) Is it possible?

NICOLE:
Yes. I am not the same! Your son gave me a life I did not deserve! I deserved better than this! I married a man who has not gone anywhere, in all these years. I got tired of waiting and waiting for a better life—better than living in this dump!

CARMELA:
But he has always given you what you need. I don't understand! I never suspected you to hold so much anger toward him!

NICOLE:
When I married Patrick, I was not expecting to marry a man that would lose his jobs as often as he changed underwear! One job after the other went by. No retirement, no home ownership! Nothing! We were never able to go on vacation to Europe! (She laughs) His land! How ironic!

PATRICK:
But there was always money for your gym, nail and beauty parlor appointments! Did you not always wear expensive clothing and cosmetics?

NICOLE:
I was your wife! You were obligated to support me in all aspects—including what was required to keep me comfortable!

CARMELA:
You have only been married six years, dear! Sometimes it takes decades to build the foundations of prosperity!

NICOLE:
Oh yeah? Well, I got fed up! I am in my thirties, and I don't intend to give up the rest of my youth to be with your loser son! That is why I am the victim! And on my channel, I encourage my followers to seek a better future. Don't conform to what others tell us to do!

(The FOLLOWERS start chanting, "Better future! Better future! Better future!")

MRS. ADELAIDE:
Better future?

(FOLLOWERS chant, "Yes! Yes! Yes!" while pointing their phones to MRS. ADELAIDE and filming her.)

MRS. ADELAIDE:
How many of you burned trailers, trashed sites? (She waits) Better yet, which one of you almost killed a man today by shooting him?

FOLLOWER 1:
Don't patronize us, old woman!

MRS. ADELAIDE:
How many of you vandalized a private property before today?

FOLLOWER 1:
I told you not to patronize us!

(FOLLOWERS approach MRS. ADELAIDE, trying to harm her. PATRICK and CARMELA walk over to her and stand right in front of her)

PATRICK:
So now you are trying to harm an old woman?

FOLLOWER 2:
To defend Nicole's and our rights! Yes!

(FOLLOWERS chant "Better future! Better future! Better future!")

NICOLE:
A woman marries a man to be given everything she needs. I am an American woman, Patrick! And you are a third-grade foreigner from a country that no one has ever heard of! I gave you the citizenship to this country-the opportunity to be with a woman like me! I gave you three children! What about you? You gave me nothing!

(TRACY enters the scene with the three children.)

TRACY:
I want you to repeat that in front of your three children! Why don't you repeat all that you've just said?

NICOLE:
Don't make me laugh, Tracy! You always envied me! (She laughs) I am everything you are not and never will be!

TRACY:
Trust me. You are the kind of person *no one* wants to be! At least I work and provide for my family! Not like you, almighty Nicole Razor, who feels entitled to be supported by others. Now repeat what you said. That Patrick gave you nothing! What about your children?

NICOLE:
(Tenderly) Come, come, my babies! Come to me!

(The three children run to NICOLE and hug her.)

CHILDREN
(TOGETHER) Mommy! Mommy! Mommy!

TRACY:
Children, come here!

MRS. ADELAIDE:
Let them, Tracy. Let it be. She is their mother, after all!

CARMELA:
Why have the police not arrived yet?

TRACY:
I am wondering the same thing, Carmela!

FOLLOWER 1:
Because we blocked the two main ways to Divinity Street. We are united throughout the network! (Referring to NICOLE) Nicole, get out with the children now!

(FOLLOWERS flank Nicole and the children toward the door and they exit the apartment)

CARMELA:
(Desperately) Patrick! The children!

PATRICK:
My children! Get out of my way!

(He walks toward the FOLLOWERS, when two of them hold his arms, while another one hits him twice, knocking him to the floor.)

CARMELA:
Mrs. Adelaide, what can we do?

FOLLOWER 2:
Nothing. You already know what we're capable of. If we hear that any of you get close to Nicole and the children, there will be consequences.

MRS. ADELAIDE:
Are you capable of killing?

FOLLOWER 1:
If it is necessary, yes.

MRS. ADELAIDE:
I see you all are a herd of sheep who follows anyone that comes in your path! Oh, poor little souls!

(FOLLOWER 1 raises his right arm and tries to slap MRS. ADELAIDE's face.)

MRS. ADELAIDE:
(Powerful) Stop it this instant!

(FOLLOWER 1 leaves arm suspended in the air for few seconds. He appears to be frozen.)

FOLLOWER 3:
Come on! Let's get out of here! We got what we came for!

FOLLOWER 2:
No! These people are going to learn the biggest lesson of their entire lives tonight!

MRS. ADELAIDE:
Come, Carmela! (The two women hold hands and start whispering prayers. PATRICK and TRACY join them in forming a circle, while the followers try to break

it by force. Then, all of a sudden, the followers appear to be zapped by an electric current every time they try to touch the circle.)

FOLLOWER 1:
(Referring to the rest of the FOLLOWERS) Take any valuables. They belong to Nicole! Just trash the rest! (FOLLOWER 1 laughs while the FOLLOWERS try to take and destroy the items, but they appear to be momentarily paralyzed.)

FOLLOWER 1:
(Referring to the rest of the FOLLOWERS) Why did you stop?

FOLLOWER 3:
I can't move!

FOLLOWER 1:
What are you talking about? Let me try! (FOLLOWER 1 tries to toss a book unsuccessfully.)

(All of a sudden, chants are heard through the window and from outside

Pariahcalais Version	Spanish Version
Lae vife es ua susght	La vida es como un suspiro
Noe espeit much dof esh	Esperamos mucho de ella
Pet at find,	Pero al final,
es thel art dof viavel	es el arte de viajar

sinout equige	sin equipaje
Ynd llerrive at destine	Y llegar al destino
Sinout herwound algume	sin herida alguna.
Pariahcalais	Pariahcalais
Pariahcalais	Pariahcalais
Pariahcalais	Pariahcalais

FOLLOWER 3:
(With a big smile on his face, FOLLOWER 3 looks through the window.) Are we expecting more of us, guys? There are more of us outside!

(PATRICK and CARMELA start singing the chant as well.)

FOLLOWER 1:
Shut up! Shut-Ooh! Ooh! (FOLLOWER 1 behaves as though he cannot finish the words, almost as if there is a piece of tape holding his mouth shut.)

FOLLOWER 3:
I think we should leave!

(All FOLLOWERS retreat in the closest corner to the exit. They all appear frantic as if they cannot move their mouths. Then they leave the scene while a uniform humming is heard simultaneously.)

CARMELA:
Is it over, Mrs. Adelaide?

MRS. ADELAIDE:
What do you think?

CARMELA:
Yes, it's over.

MRS. ADELAIDE:
It's over, indeed!

(BOTH women laugh and hug)

TRACY:
What is over?

PATRICK:
(Laughs) I think I know what!

TRACY:
I don't understand. Nicole got the children, you lost your workplace, they almost trashed your home . . . and you all laugh?

MRS. ADELAIDE:
Tracy,
Life is as brief as a sigh.
We expect much of it,
but at the end . . .
It's the art of traveling
without luggage
and arriving to the destination
without any injuries!

CARMELA:
That is what life is about!

TRACY:
I don't get what you're saying. Does this have something to do with the spell?

PATRICK:
Yes! There was indeed a spell, once upon a time. It was intended to destroy my ancestors and my future generations. I believed that running away from Pariahcalais was the solution, the escape from the problem, but I was mistaken.

TRACY:
But Patrick, Joshua has lost everything, and we do not have our jobs anymore!

PATRICK:
That is true, but now I have peace in my heart. The one I have longed and always dreamed of Tracy. I am finally free! For the first time, I don't fear anything!
(He laughs, then hugs TRACY)

CARMELA:
There is more action against adversities with inactions, Tracy! It takes courage and strength. Let's take a palm tree on a deserted island, for example. A

tsunami wipes the entire place as strong winds try to bend its leaves, trunk and core. The core is close to being rotten after having been under the water for days. The palm tree cannot move; it is attached to the earth. But after a few weeks, when most of the land has dried out, the palm tree stands intact—healthier and stronger than ever—giving us the most juicy and beautiful coconuts that we can dream of!

MRS. ADELAIDE:
And this palm tree that our dear Carmela has described, has probably endured countless tsunamis before. And still, it stands throughout many years. Ah, by the way . . . (She holds one of TRACY'S and PATRICK'S arms) You two still have a job!

TRACY:
What are you talking about?

MRS. ADELAIDE:
I am actually one of your bosses!

TRACY and PATRICK:
What?

MRS. ADELAIDE:
Yes, yes, yes, my dears . . . (Chuckles) Let me tell you. Years ago, I met Joshua Harris, Nathaniel Davis, and

Benign Williams. At the time, I owned a stand in the farmers market—a rather successful stand by the way! I made the most delicious falafel in the entire place. I made it from scratch and with tons of love. One day, I was preparing to lock the door, when these three big guys pointed a gun at my head. You can just imagine the terror I felt then.

TRACY:
What? I never heard about this!

MRS. ADELAIDE:
Yes. Although I was powerless, I was younger and more alert. At the time, I had a big jar of fermented cabbage with carrots lying on top of the counter. I ducked, squeezed myself, crawled among their legs and reached the counter. Without thinking much, I grabbed the jar, opened it, and threw the cabbage to their face. You see, the vinegar stung their eyes, and that's when I grabbed their gun! I took the bullets out and simply left.

PATRICK:
Left? You didn't call the police?

MRS. ADELAIDE:
No. I did better than that; I prayed.

TRACY:
What happened after?

(BENIGN opens the door and enters the scene)

BENIGN:
I'll tell you! We wanted to kill her. So Nathaniel got more bullets from his truck, and we waited for her behind the counter and pointed the gun at her. Do you want to know what she did next?

TRACY and PATRICK:
What?

BENIGN:
Nothing. She kept walking, left her purse on top of the counter, took a broom, and gave it to Joshua. She commanded him to start sweeping the mess we made the night before. Then, I asked Joshua why he was doing what she said, but he kept sweeping. In that moment, Mrs. Adelaide stood up in front of the three of us and asked us if we wanted to work for her.

(TRACY and PATRICK laugh)

BENIGN:
I felt so many feelings throughout my body. I wanted to kill this woman, to destroy her, to burn the dump she owned, but at the same time, I felt puzzled by this weird fuzzy feeling that spread

through all my body. She asked us what we were good at besides committing crimes and getting high. Joshua mentioned he was good at using concrete, so Mrs. Adelaide told us that she would hire us to build little projects in exchange for us giving up our lives in crime and drugs.

PATRICK:
Did it work?

BENIGN:
Oh, no. It did not work. You see, man, we showed up to work so freaking high that we left the site without doing anything. And when we worked, we used the money we made to buy more drugs. Nathaniel went back to jail for possession. It was a mess. Interesting thing though, Mrs. Adelaide never fussed at us, man! Then something started to happen . . . we heard that a lot of the ex-convicts on parole were looking to work for her, so Joshua, Nath and I decided that we were going to try harder and get better. And after a few years, we actually did it, man! We got better. The three of us have got families to support. And since then, we have tried to live a decent life for the

last twenty years. All thanks to Mrs.
Adelaide, here. But I'll tell you, it's
a constant struggle.

MRS. ADELAIDE:
Tracy and Patrick, when these three
gentleman—among others—started to
get serious about life, all of them
worked hard and saved a significant
amount of money to invest in our little
construction crew. We created a sort of
legitimate association—a cooperative—in
which all of us could own a piece of the
business. We designated Mr. Joshua as
the acting manager. And the rest dear
kids, is history. Now, I don't have
to work anymore. (She laughs) I am a
retired old woman, but I love cooking,
so I'll still have my street food cart.

PATRICK:
But Mrs. Adelaide, the site was destroyed; we don't have the equipment to
resume the construction.

BENIGN:
My man! Don't you worry. We have our
cushion fund. We will be fine! I may add,
ex-convicts live life in constant battle. We want to do wrong. It's inside
us, man. But all criminals have a certain standard of ethics. You know what

I'm saying? One called the villains' crew road code of ethics. No matter how rotten we are, that code is always there!

TRACY:
But Bennie . . . why the secrecy about Mrs. Adelaide's role in the company?

MRS. ADELAIDE:
I wanted to be less involved. In that way, I could keep an eye on them without being in the way.

PATRICK:
Wow, Tracy. I never suspected that the place you brought me over to work was so colorful! (He laughs)

MRS. ADELAIDE:
The same palm tree principle applies for the rest of the crew and everybody. Now, changing the subject! (Referring to BENIGN) Have you heard anything about Joshie's condition?

BENIGN:
Oh, yes! He is in the ICU but he's safe.

(ALL make sounds of relief)

MRS. ADELAIDE:
Carmela, what were those chants earlier from outside?

CARMELA:
I don't know how, but it was one of our national chants!

TRACY:
Ah, yes. Someone texted and told me when your ex-wife's followers were filming the whole thing. Some of your country's men gathered outside the building to sing.

CARMELA:
Oh . . . it was magical!

MRS. ADELAIDE:
Indeed, dear Carmela! I feel it is going to be time for you to return to your land very soon.

CARMELA:
Yes.

TRACY:
Have you all forgotten something of major importance in all this chaos?

CARMELA:
Do you mean my grandkids?

TRACY:
Exactly! The children. They were kidnapped!

PATRICK:
Not really, Tracy.

TRACY:
I saw it!

PATRICK:
We never put up any legal paperwork to make our separation official. She has every right to take the kids.

TRACY:
I can't believe what you are saying, Patrick. That woman was among a bunch of people that committed vandalism, arson, almost killed Joshua, trespassed private properties . . . not to mention assault! She cannot have those kids! If you won't call DHR, I will.

CARMELA:
Everything you are saying is right, Tracy. But those are her kids. Maybe it will do well for her to take some responsibility and spend some alone time with them. She was not always as she is now. She used to be more caring.

MRS. ADELAIDE:
Tracy, dear, what happened here tonight had to happen.

CARMELA:
The spell will always be there. But tonight, Patrick and I felt the freedom and peace that comes from inside us; an acceptance which I now know will be rewarded from now on.

(Someone knocks on the door)

POLICEMAN:
(from outside) Police! Open the door!

(PATRICK approaches, opening the door. The POLICEMAN enters.)

POLICEMAN:
Sir! We tried to reach you earlier, but we have street blockages throughout.

PATRICK:
Yes, officer, we know.

POLICEMAN:
Is everybody all right?

PATRICK:
So far so good, sir!

POLICEMAN:
Can you give me a detailed description of the criminals?

TRACY:
Officer! I can describe the leader to you! Her name is Nic—(CARMELA holds her arm and wags her head sideways.)

POLICEMAN:
Yes ma'am, go ahead.

TRACY:
Well, now that I think about it, I am not sure . . . All I can say is that there were a bunch of a so-called "TooYube channel" followers.

POLICEMAN:
I'll tell you what, you are all going to come to the station to make official statements.

PATRICK:
Is that necessary, officer? My mother and Mrs. Adelaide are two elderly women. They have been through a lot tonight.

BENIGN:
Yeah, man, leave these older folks alone!

POLICEMAN:
Bennie! What the heck are you doing here? (He glances to the rest of the people.) Does he have anything to do with this?

MRS. ADELAIDE:
Oh, no officer! Benign is just a very good friend of ours.

POLICEMAN:
Oh, great! I would hate to see him in more trouble!

BENIGN:
Oh, you just don't want to miss out on the poker nights, huh? (He laughs)

POLICEMAN:
(Laughs a little) Hey, Benign, it's great to see you. But you know the drill, here! All of you have to come to headquarters. Come on.

(ALL head to the door except for PATRICK, MRS. ADELAIDE and CARMELA.)

PATRICK:
Mother! Are you going to be all right?

CARMELA:
I think so. Go! Do what the officer has asked you to do!

MRS. ADELAIDE:
Plus, I am here, son. (She gently grabs one of PATRICK'S arms, and takes him aside) What are you going to do about your wife and kids? Are you going to report the situation? A lot of details are going to come to the surface in the interrogation room.

PATRICK:
Mrs. Adelaide, I am not going to mention my wife's name. As my mother said earlier, despite the current circumstances, my ex-wife was good to me and the children. I cannot blame her for feeling frustration after so many disappointments, even though most of them were out of my hands.

MRS. ADELAIDE:
There is always the Fifth Amendment, you know. Sooner or later, she will be brought for questioning.

PATRICK:
I'll worry about it then, Mrs. Adelaide. In the meantime, stay here and don't open the door for anyone!

CARMELA:
Go, son! Go!

(PATRICK leaves the scene.)

MRS. ADELAIDE:
Carmela, are you really willing to forget about what happened with your daughter-in-law tonight?

CARMELA:
Oh, what do we get in making the problem bigger than it is? After all, you and I know this whole situation and many more in the past have been collateral results of a distant damage.

MRS. ADELAIDE:
(Hold hands with CARMELA) My friend! I have waited so long to see you again!

CARMELA:
Nose heve vuelmet a encontramet otragain!
We have met again!

MRS. ADELAIDE:
Yoi lo sanewt!
I knew it!

(The scene turns dark. One soft-white spotlight is directed at the two women. Purple and blue lights are aimed at a group of people dressed in white tunics when they open the door. They hold a long white transparent sheet of cloth while approaching MRS. ADELAIDE and CARMELA. They circle around the pair, while holding the sheet. Then, raise their arms, as they approach CARMELA and MRS. ADELAIDE, and cover them with the cloth while singing the

Pariahcalais chant sang earlier. After five slow circles, the circle opens as a concave shape toward the audience. The scene turns completely dark while NICOLE and her three children enter the scene. A soft-white spotlight aims at these four characters. The three children are hugging their mother while crying. Simultaneously, another soft-white spotlight aims at MRS. ADELAIDE and CARMELA. CARMELA opens her arms to receive the children while they walk toward her. NICOLE remains behind, looking embarrassed and sobbing. Once the children have reached Carmela's hands, they remain frozen for a few seconds. Then CARMELA walks toward NICOLE, grabs her hands and walks with her to reach MRS. ADELAIDE and the children.)

(The spotlight that was aiming at NICOLE and the children follows them all along to unify in one unique dim, soft-white light. This light covers the two elderly women, NICOLE, and the children.)

(All soft-white spotlights dim. The purple and blue lights aim at the people in white tunics while they close the circle again. They sing the Pariahcalais one more time, while completing the last loop to finish in whispers. All lights dim.)

THE END

The Business Park

THE BUSINESS PARK

Cast:

Mateo Naranja
Oscar
Mariona Goddard
Jessie Mercedes
Rick Vines
Bin Cheapbarr
Tom Larvhaz
Mrs. Larvhaz
Dave Montgomery
Savina
Lili
Helper 1 (Louis)
Helper 2
Customer 1
Petro
Justo Fidel

(The scene consists of two pop-up tent stands. Each stand has a chair, a table with a blender and a pile of plastic cups on top, and a big showroom table with crates filled with fruits. One of the stands sells tomatoes, while the other sells oranges. The latter has a big sign which reads: Naranja Enterprises, LLC, while the other one reads: Larvhaz Dutch Tomatoes. Between the two stands, there is a counter bar with a sign that reads: Cheapbarr Enterprises, and a visible messy pile of boxes behind. Between the proscenium and the counter bar, there is a medium-size park bench facing the audience at a forty-five-degree angle.

(At the oranges stand labeled Naranja Enterprises, MATEO sits, punching numbers in an old, gigantic calculator. He is tall, skinny, and bald, wearing a long necklace with a big cross.)

MATEO:
Ave Purisima, Concebida, Del Gran Padre Todo poderoso! (Makes the Catholic symbol of the Cross.) I can't believe I have to pay five bucks for that DARN food Savina sells me! Mateo . . . Imagine all the money you can save, if only I

made it myself . . . Hm . . . I am going to call her! In fact, I'll call right now! Five dollars? (He scoffs.) How ridiculous! Hm!

(OSCAR, his assistant, enters the scene.)

MATEO:
Oscar! Why are you so late?

OSCAR:
Boss, don't you remember? After picking the oranges, down in Ocala, I went home very late last night! I barely got any sleep!

MATEO:
That's no excuse to be late!

OSCAR:
I am so sorry, boss. I promise, it won't happen again.

MATEO:
Oh! Hush your mouth. Now, listen, have you seen Savina, lately?

OSCAR:
No . . . Why?

MATEO:
Her food really gives me the vapors, if you know what I mean. It is so expensive! Can you believe she raised her prices from $4.25 to $5.00?

OSCAR:
Boss, she has been charging $4.25 for the

last ten years. Don't you think it was about time she raised her prices? After all, she always gives you lechon asado, rice with beans and maduro, with a bonus of lemon coleslaw. (Pause) Ah! Now that I think about it . . . I know now, what gives you the vapors, boss.

MATEO:
Boy, what are you talking about?

OSCAR:
Well . . . the combination of beans and coleslaw . . . can be rather explosive. No wonder why—

(MATEO interrupts him, abruptly.)

MATEO:
Ah! Hush now and go back to work this instant!

OSCAR:
Yes, sir! (Exits the scene.)

(While MATEO paces around, he looks at his phone intensely, and approaches it to dial.)

MATEO:
Hello? Is Mrs. Mariona Goddard there? Ah! Is it you? Hello Mariona, it's Mateo Naranja, the proud owner of Naranja Enterprises, LLC. Yes? Oh yes! Listen, I was wondering—how much do you charge

for the full plate of lechon asado? Uh-huh . . . Uh-huh . . . Yes? *How* much? It's impossible! That's too much, Mariona. I don't think I will be doing business with you, ma'am! (Pauses, listening.) Okay? I am all ears. Ah, I see . . . (Brief pause) Now we're talking! Can you bring it to my tent today? Great. Then it's a deal, ma'am! See you then. Bye (He hangs up.) Yes, yes, yes!

(MATEO laughs and jumps. OSCAR enters the scene.)

OSCAR:
Boss, did you win Bingo at the Eustis Community Center?

MATEO:
No—even better! Do you know Mariona Goddard? The one who owns the food truck? (Oscar nods.) She is going to sell me lechon for three dollars; it comes with avocado, beans, rice, tostones, and you're not going to believe what else.

OSCAR:
(Confused) What else, boss?

MATEO:
Flan! (Laughs)

OSCAR:
But boss, Savina is going through a very rough patch. She can't even afford the food truck that Mariona Goddard owns!

MATEO:
That's not my problem!

OSCAR:
Did you tell Savina already?

MATEO:
Heck, no! Let her find out for herself.

OSCAR:
But boss, she's probably already on her way to deliver your food!

MATEO:
Oscar . . . Do you see this cross? (Points at a necklace he is wearing, then solemnly continues.) I pray every day, and He knows my actions are justified.

OSCAR:
(Hesitates) Well, you are the boss, after all. You know better . . . I guess?

MATEO:
Stop wasting time! And go to Tavares, to pick up the grapefruits for the jelly! Remember? The nuns at the convent ordered those grapefruits last week. Andele! Andele!

OSCAR:
Can you give me some money for gas? Ah! And some for a yummy sausage . . . Some pork rinds, maybe?

MATEO:
Oh . . . (Fake cough) I am a little short of cash now. Maybe tomorrow? Yes, tomorrow!

OSCAR:
Boss, you always say that.

(MATEO remains awkwardly quiet and turns the volume up on his radio.)

OSCAR:
Okay, boss. I'm leaving!

MATEO:
Oh yes! Fly! Fly like the wind. Go, go, go!

(OSCAR exits. MATEO sits and pushes the buttons of his calculator while soft music plays. Meanwhile, TOM LARVHAZ, owner of Larvhaz Dutch Tomatoes, the tomato stand, checks his tomatoes. One by one, he examines and smells them. Suddenly, he spots MATEO and approaches him.)

TOM:
Hello, there!

MATEO:
(Stands up) Hello Tom, to what do I owe the honor?

TOM:
Have you had the chance to order those bitter oranges I requested, some time ago?

MATEO:
You know . . . God is so good to me! (Chuckles) I just got two orders, big enough to cover my expenses for the next two years! Hallelujah!

TOM:
(Challenging) Do you mean, you won't bother with my bitter oranges? Is it what you are saying, Naranja?

MATEO:
Oh, no! You misunderstood me. For you, my friend, I'll do the impossible!

TOM:
So, when can I expect them? I need them for my new line of tomato-based rubs. You know, for the upcoming Cheapbarr Festival!

MATEO:
Of course, of course. Give me a couple of days. I promise, you'll have your bitter oranges!

TOM:
(Takes his wallet, opens it, and shows the contents to MATEO.) Do I need to show you my wallet? (MATEO appears confused.) Look! (MATEO looks closely.) I hope, now that you have seen the money, you will hurry with my order!

MATEO:
Oh, yes! You will have it, you will have it. No worries!

TOM:
Okay, I hope so!

(TOM returns to his tomato stand.)

MATEO:
(To himself) You won't be in the Cheapbarr Festival. You should be in the Cheapskate festival . . . (Looks up) God, forgive me! Oh Lord, I am so good! (Sits to keep punching numbers in his calculator.)

(SAVINA enters the scene, carrying a plastic box with MATEO's lunch inside. She looks very tired and wipes away the sweat running down her forehead. She remains between the tomato and orange stands. Then MARIONA enters the scene, carrying a box of food as well.)

MARIONA:
Ah, Savina. You're here?

SAVINA:
Oh, hello Mrs. Goddard! Yes, I am here with Mr. Naranja's lunch. (Giggles)

MARIONA:
What did you just say?

SAVINA:
That I am here with Mr. Naranja's lunch. Food . . . grub? (Weak laugh)

MARIONA:
Well, well. That is rather ridiculous! I am here with Mr. Naranja's lunch, myself!

SAVINA:
But—but . . . I don't understand. What do you mean?

MARIONA:
Why don't we go and ask him, shall we?

(SAVINA nods and both walk toward Mateo's stand.)

MARIONA:
Hello, Mr. Naranja? I am Mariona Goddard.

MATEO:
(Stands up) Oh! Call me Mateo, please.

MARIONA:
Okay, Mateo. This young woman says she's here with your food. *I* am here with your food. I am HERE with YOUR FOOD!

MATEO:
Of course, of course. (Chuckles)

SAVINA:
Mr. Naranja, what do you mean by, "of course?"

(While MATEO ignores SAVINA, he takes money from his wallet.)

MATEO:
Here, Mrs. Goddard, why don't I give you an advance for the rest of the month? (Hands MARIONA the money.) You can count it if you want! Your outstanding reputation is enough. I can just imagine the fine taste of your vittles!

MARIONA:
Oh! That won't be necessary. I trust you, Mateo. Thank you! (Gives the lunch box to MATEO.) I'll be here tomorrow at the same time. Thank you for your business (Both shake hands. She waves her hand.) Ciao, Ciao! (Exits)

SAVINA:
Mr. Naranja, what should I do with your lunch box?

MATEO:
Are you talking to me, ma'am?

SAVINA:
Well . . . yes, who else would I be talking to?

MATEO:
You should give it to the owner of the pig farm, down Indian River. Now please, let me be. I am a very busy man!

SAVINA:
Mr. Naranja, I have brought your lunch boxes for the last ten years. You know my father needs the money to run his okra farm. Doesn't that mean anything to you?

MATEO:
(Stands up) Child! When a king is dethroned, a new one is crowned! (Solemnly) It hurts my soul, child, but Mrs. Goddard has been just recently crowned, here at Naranja Enterprises. Do you get it? (SAVINA nods) Well, now . . . If you'll excuse me, I am very busy, so—scoot, scoot!

(SAVINA appears confused and leaves MATEO's stand and walks to the middle of the stage. TOM walks towards her.)

TOM:
Are you okay?

SAVINA:
I think so . . .

TOM:
Did the Naranja guy do something to you?

SAVINA:
No . . . it doesn't matter. I am just heading home.

TOM:
(Eager) I can take you home; I have a very spacious Mercedes Bench!

SAVINA:
That won't be necessary, Mr. Larvhaz.

TOM:
How many times have I asked you to call me Tom?

SAVINA:
(Giggles) I know. It's out of respect. After all, you are my father's friend.

TOM:
That doesn't mean you have to call *me* by my last name.

SAVINA:
Well . . . maybe you're right, Mr. Larvhaz—I mean—Tom. Yes, Tom!

TOM:
My name sounds so special, coming from your sweet lips.

SAVINA:
(Giggles) Oh, Tom. I think I'll accept your generous offer for a ride home, after all.

TOM:
That's my girl! Come then, after you. (Indicates her to walk in front of him)

(Both exit the scene, while music plays. BIN, RICK and ANTHONY enter. ANTHONY pushes an ice cream cart labeled, The Frozen Iguana. The three men walk toward the bar counter, taking positions behind it as they quietly talk.)

RICK:
Bin, when are you going to clear out this mess here? (Points to the boxes behind the counter.)

BIN:
I'll tell you what . . . when I find someone to do it for me; that's for sure!

ANTHONY:
Where am I supposed to put The Frozen Iguana cart, huh?

BIN:
What do you mean? We have not talked about numbers yet.

ANTHONY:
Ooh . . . numbers! My favorites: why don't we eat some ice cream before? Huh? (Lifts the lid of the cart to give popsicles to the other two men.) With ice cream, everything is better! (Laughs)

BIN:
Boy, you are right! (He unwraps the popsicle and eats it.) Mmm . . . yummy!

RICK:
And the best of all . . . They are free! I hope . . . (He chuckles) But seriously, Mr. Creamery. Next time, we want to see you paying rent like the rest of us in this park! (Aside, whispers) Supposedly...

ANTHONY:
You got it!

(While all men laugh, the Mayor DAVE MONTGOMERY enters the scene wearing a lilac-colored T-shirt.)

DAVE:
Mr. Cheapbarr. (He nods at BIN, then looks to the rest.) Howdy, y'all!

BIN:
There he is! (He shakes hands with DAVE.)

DAVE:
Did you guys see the game last night?

RICK:
Oh, man! I can't believe what they did.

ANTHONY:
Man . . . That was suicide!

DAVE:
Why do you think I am wearing this shirt today? Huh?

ANTHONY:
I thought someone died in your family . . . there was a death in the family. (He laughs)

BIN:
Of course someone died, Anthony . . . The opposing team! (All laugh except Dave.)

DAVE:
This is the color of serenity. It's the color of the calm that only the winners can experience while the losers, well . . . How would I put it? While they SUCK IT! (Laughs hard)

(All laugh)

RICK:
Mayor, are you here for the festival?

DAVE:
Folks, it appears Rick here, just wants to go straight to the serious business, huh?

RICK:
Yes. I already have to deal with Mr. Creamery's popsicles here, if you know what I mean?

DAVE:
What's that supposed to mean? What the heck are you talking about?

ANTHONY:
(Laughs) Everything is better with ice cream!

RICK:
What will make things better for you, Mr. Creamery, is to pay your part of the tab!

BIN:
Rick, don't you worry about that. I will surely keep diligent track of Mr. Creamery's bill. Don't you worry, boy! (The three men start arguing.)

DAVE:
Boys! I didn't come from up yonder to hear about business conflicts. I came here to talk about the famous Cheapbarr Festival!

BIN:
Ah, yes . . . The Cheapbarr Festival. What about it, Mayor?

DAVE:
Now we're talking! I have the list of all the vendors' information and their payments for their tables—except for you, Mr. Creamery.

ANTHONY:
Oh! Don't worry, you'll have it!

RICK & BIN:
When?

ANTHONY:
Soon . . . soon . . . (Laughs)

DAVE:
Well . . . Enough said, Mr. Creamery, you'll have until tonight to pay your submission.

ANTHONY:
(Solemnly) Mayor, you have my word.

DAVE:
I heard that! Well, my boss, well . . . that is, my wife, if you know what I mean . . . is waiting for me to get us some barbecue; so . . . See you, boys!

(All men shake hands and DAVE leaves the scene.)

RICK:
So, Bin, when are you going to clear this mess? I need space to pile my grape crates.

BIN:
I told you, I need to find someone to clear it out for me.

RICK:
Ain't twenty years been enough for you?

BIN:
I am a businessman. I don't do that kind of thing.

RICK:
I hear you. Well, then find someone!

ANTHONY:
What about that boy? The one who helps Mateo Naranja at his stand?

BIN:
Oh . . . You're right . . .

ANTHONY:
Now we're talking!

RICK:
What are you waiting for? Go, talk to him! Go!

BIN:
Okay, partner, okay.

(BIN walks towards MATEO's stand)

BIN:
Hey! There he is!

MATEO:
Mr. Cheapbarr!

BIN:
Howdy, neighbor. How are we doing?

MATEO:
Great! Like never before.

BIN:
Good to hear that, good to hear that.

MATEO:
To what do I owe the honor of your presence, in this humble establishment?

BIN:
(Laughs)
Humble? This place is a success for the community!

MATEO:
Oh, no . . . Yours is a success!

BIN:
Amen.

MATEO:
Thanks to the Lord above.

BIN:
Amen.

MATEO:
What can I do for you, Mr. Cheapbarr?

BIN:
Does that boy . . . hmm . . . your helper—is he still around?

MATEO:
Oh, yes. He is. Any special reason, you ask?

BIN:
Well, I need someone to help move some clutter out of my business.

MATEO:
Oh . . . It was about time!

BIN:
What did you just say?

MATEO:
Oh! What better time than *now*, is what I said.

BIN:
Ah! Anyhow, is that boy available to help me out? I can pay him, of course.

MATEO:
Now that I think about it, you can actually pay *me* directly. After all, he is my employee and will do . . . (Chuckles) what I tell him to do.

BIN:
I could care less who I pay, as long as he clears out the mess.

MATEO:
Of course! (Laughs)

BIN:
I heard that. Well . . . when can he start?

MATEO:
I'll send the boy your way as soon he comes back from Tavares.

BIN:
Excellent! I'll be waiting, then.

MATEO:
It's a pleasure!

(Both men shake hands. While BIN walks towards the bar counter, JESSIE enters the scene. He is wearing a suit and tie.)

JESSIE:
Good morning, gentlemen.

RICK/BIN/ANTHONY:
Good morning!

BIN:
There he is.

JESSIE:
Mr. Celebrity Cheapbarr! It's so good to see you!

BIN:
Mr. Mercedes. To what do we owe the honor?

JESSIE:
I'm actually looking for Mr. Tom Larvhaz. Have any of you seen him?

(BIN, RICK, and ANTHONY wag their heads)

JESSIE:
What a shame!

ANTHONY:
Ice cream, Mr. Mercedes?

JESSIE:
Oh, no thanks.

RICK:
Didn't you sell him the brand-new car Tom is driving, now?

JESSIE:
Ah, yes.

RICK:
That there's quite an expensive ride he got himself, huh?

JESSIE:
Indeed. *Quite* expensive!

RICK:
I guess tomatoes are selling well these days, huh?

BIN:
Hmm . . . I guess . . .

(OSCAR enters the scene carrying a heavy box of grapefruit. JESSIE moves to a corner of the stage and starts quietly talking on his phone.)

BIN:
Hey, boy!

OSCAR:
(Confused) Yes? How are you, sir?

BIN:
Hmm . . . sure. Have you talked to your boss, yet?

OSCAR:
No, why?

BIN:
Well, you better go and talk to him, boy.

OSCAR:
Is there something wrong?

BIN:
No. After you talk to your boss, come back right away!

OSCAR:
Come back here? Why?

BIN:
You just do what I say, boy.

OSCAR:
Okay? (Walks towards MATEO) Boss, I am here!

MATEO:
How are the grapefruits?

OSCAR:
Well, see for yourself.

MATEO:
(Examines them) They appear to be fine. Go warm up the stove, then.

OSCAR:
But . . .

MATEO:
But *what*, boy? What?

OSCAR:
The guy from the bar told me to talk to you, then go back there. Do you know why?

MATEO:
Oh, yes! Go back and do what he tells you to do!

OSCAR:
But . . .

MATEO:
Again with the buts? Go! And do what he *tells* you to do!

OSCAR:
I don't understand. I don't work for him, you know?

MATEO:
Yes, yes. He asked to borrow you—to help him clear some mess.

OSCAR:
Why me? Why doesn't he do it himself?

MATEO:
Boy! How dare you? He is a businessman like me.

OSCAR:
But . . .

MATEO:
Go now, boy!

OSCAR:
Okay . . . I guess it's fine? (Walks toward BIN's bar counter.)

OSCAR:
Sir, my boss told me to come help you?

BIN:
Oh, yes. Do you see those boxes? (OSCAR nods) Open all of them and sort them out.

OSCAR:
Okay? (Confused)

BIN:
Boy! Don't you understand English?

OSCAR:
Yes, sir.

BIN:
Well?

ANTHONY:
Here. (To OSCAR) Have a Popsicle!

OSCAR:
Thanks. (He walks away and starts clearing the mess.)

RICK:
I'm going to bring in some of the grape crates while the young man cleans that mess.

BIN:
Sounds like a plan!

(RICK exits)

BIN:
So, Mr. Mercedes, is everything okay here?

JESSIE:
(Puts his hand over his phone) I'm just waiting for Tom—if that's okay with you, of course?

BIN:
Oh, yes! That's fine. Would you like to try some of Rick Vine's muscadine wine?

JESSIE:
Is it Merlot? Chardonnay? Moscato, perhaps?

BIN:
Mr. Mercedes, you know your wines, huh? (Both men laugh) No, it is muscadine, as I said before.

JESSIE:
Is it a sample?

BIN:
Why not? A sample it is! (Takes a bottle and serves him wine in a plastic cup.) There! (JESSIE takes a sip) Well? What do you think?

JESSIE:
It is . . . adequate, I guess.

BIN:
Oh . . . okay? (Awkward pause) Did you say you need to see Tom? (JESSIE nods) I'm actually working in a partnership with Tom for a new beverage!

JESSIE:
Oh?

BIN:
Yes! He is such a great businessman.

JESSIE:
I suppose so. However, I would not think good businessmen are late with their payments when they purchase their goods.

BIN:
How so? Is he late on any of his payments?

JESSIE:
Mr. Tom Larvhaz hasn't been making his new Mercedes Bench payments on time, if you know what I mean.

BIN:
Is that so?

JESSIE:
Uh-huh.

BIN:
What I don't understand is . . . what does that have to do with me?

JESSIE:
Well, you just said you'd be working in some sort of partnership with him?

BIN:
Sir, I am going to stop you right there—

JESSIE:
You can't. You see, when people don't pay what they owe me, I always find a way to get my money back.

BIN:
Is that a threat?

JESSIE:
Take it as you wish, Cheapbarr.

BIN:
Mister, I am going to insist you leave right now!

JESSIE:
Ah . . . not so friendly, anymore? What a shame. (Approaches BIN) A little word of advice, Cheapbarr: if I were you, I would be *very* careful about whom I choose to do my business.

(Walks out of the scene)

BIN:
(Appears thoughtful—talks to OSCAR, who has stopped to lean on a pile of boxes while wiping sweat from his brow.) How are things here?

OSCAR:
I am trying to do my best, sir.

BIN:
If you got time to lean, you got time clean, boy. I'd try harder if I was you.

OSCAR:
Sure thing, sir.

(RICK enters the scene carrying a crate full of grapes.)

RICK:
I'm here! Hasn't that boy finished, yet?

BIN:
(Shakes his head) Can you believe it?

RICK:
I don't have to believe it. I am actually seeing it. These young people are just plain lazy, unlike us, the older generation.

BIN:
I heard that! (To OSCAR) Finish quickly. Hurry up, boy! (Scoffs) That's why we pay you.

OSCAR:
Yes, sir.

BIN:
Hey Rick, we need to talk.

RICK:
What about?

BIN:
Well, about Tom Larvhaz.

RICK:
What about Tom Larvhaz? Is something wrong with the tomato wine?

BIN:
I think the tomato wine . . . might not be such a good idea, after all.

RICK:
What are you talking about? We're partners with him now.

BIN:
(While looking out, BIN grabs RICK away from where OSCAR is working.) Mr. Mercedes just informed me that Larvhaz owes him money for his new ride.

RICK:
So?

BIN:
Mercedes hinted, he would try to get his money through our partnership, *if* you know what I mean.

RICK:
Oh . . . Now I see. Well . . . we are done with Mr. Larvhaz, then.

BIN:
What about our investment?

RICK:
Let's return it to him and be done! I don't want anything to do with him anymore.

BIN:
Just like that?

RICK:
It pains me, Bin, but we are businessmen. We don't want to be liable for Larvhaz at any cost. The less said, the better.

BIN:
I heard that.

(MATEO approaches the scene.)

MATEO:
How are we doing here?

BIN:
Well, your boy has been just . . . adequate.

MATEO:
Is that so? Let me talk to that boy.
(Approaches OSCAR.) Oscar, I need you to finish quickly!

OSCAR:
Boss, I'm trying but this is a lot of work.

MATEO:
Boy, you must do better than this. I need you to pick up the bitter oranges for Mr. Larvhaz's rub.

OSCAR:
But, boss . . . I haven't had any rest in more than a week.

MATEO:
Boy, no whining! (Walks away while talking.) Now, hurry up!

(TOM and SAVINA enter the scene at the Larvhaz Tomato Stand.)

TOM:
I am so glad you came back with me, sweetie.

SAVINA:
Thank you, Tom. Would you like me to help you with something while I'm here?

TOM:
Oh, no. Let me finish some things and I'll take you to the waterfront restaurant.

SAVINA:
That sounds so nice, Tom. (LILI enters the scene and sits at the central bench.) Actually, do you mind if I go and talk to my friend Lili? She just came by . . .

TOM:
You can do whatever you want, baby.

(SAVINA giggles and walks towards LILI.)

SAVINA:
Lili!

LILI:
Savina, what a surprise! (Both hug.) How are you, girl?

SAVINA:
Great! I'm just great.

LILI:
I'm so glad! But . . . what are you doing here?

SAVINA:
Oh yes . . . that . . .

LILI:
What I mean is . . . How did you make it here?

SAVINA:
Well . . . Tom brought me over.

LILI:
Tom? Tom Larvhaz?

SAVINA:
Yes, Tom . . .

LILI:
Okay? But— (SAVINA interrupts her.)

SAVINA:
Do you still work for Mrs. Mariona Goddard?

LILI:
Who, me? Oh . . . Heck no! I lost my job because of *her*.

SAVINA:
Really? How come? Did she fire you?

LILI:
No. (Laughs) She can't fire anyone. She isn't the owner, you know?

SAVINA:
Is that so? I was under the impression she owned the food truck.

LILI:
Oh, no! She is the business manager.

SAVINA:
So, how come you lost your job because of her, then?

LILI:
Girl . . . To make the story short, I am just going to tell you that there were complaints about orders deliveried late. Well, the woman decided to blame *me* for that. Consequently, the real owner fired me.

SAVINA:
Oh, no! I'm so sorry, Lili.

LILI:
Oh . . . don't be, Savina. I've actually opened my own business.

SAVINA:
Really?

LILI:
Oh yes. My husband and I just opened a coffee and deli shop down in Deltona.

SAVINA:
That's so awesome, Lili! So, what are you doing here?

LILI:
I came to pick up some bottles of wine from Mr. Rick Vines' Wines.

SAVINA:
Yes, it's great wine!

LILI:
Yes, it is indeed . . . Do you know he has stands in different places across Central Florida?

SAVINA:
No . . . I didn't know.

LILI:
Yes . . . he does.

SAVINA:
Well, I better go back to Tom's stand.

LILI:
Savina, I wouldn't be hanging around that guy, if I was you.

SAVINA:
What guy? (Nervously, as if she's been caught.)

LILI:
Oh, don't play goofy with me, girl. You know he's married, right?

SAVINA:
No . . . is that so?

LILI:
Oh yes . . . His wife lives in Orlando, and that's not all . . . he's been messing around with none other than Mariona Goddard for some time now.

SAVINA:
(Emotional) What?

LILI:
Yes! Stay away from him, please.

(SAVINA appears to be very disappointed.)

LILI:
Oh no, Savina, don't be sad!

SAVINA:
Oh no! It's because . . . well . . . your revelation took me by surprise.

LILI:
What can I say? And I warn you! When things ended with Mariona, he really treated her like trailer trash.

SAVINA:
(Sobbing) I can't believe it.

(RICK approaches the two with a bag of a few bottles of wine.)

RICK:
Hello, Lili. I assume you came by to pick up your order?

LILI:
You got it, Mr. Vines.

RICK:
Here, take this.

LILI:
Thank you, Mr. Vines.

RICK:
Please, give my regards to your hubby.

LILI:
I sure will.

(RICK goes back to the counter bar.)

LILI:
Savina, I'll give you a ride home!

SAVINA:
That sounds great. Thank you! Just give me a second to tell Tom.

LILI:
No . . . No . . . Let's go, *now*! He doesn't deserve anything from you!

SAVINA:
But— (LILI abruptly grabs one of her arms and both leave the scene.)

(TOM walks towards the bench and appears confused while looking around for SAVINA. He stands briefly when BIN approaches him to talk.)

BIN:
Tom! Are you okay?

TOM:
What? Oh, yes. Say, have you seen a young girl? She was around this bench, earlier.

BIN:
No . . . why?

TOM:
That's strange . . .

BIN:
Anyhow, Tom, we've got to talk!

TOM:
(Arrogantly) What do you want?

BIN:
(Signals TOM to follow him.) Step into my office, please. (Both men head over to the counter bar.)

TOM:
Well? What's up?

RICK:
Mr. Larvhaz, there are some rumors going around that quite frankly . . . make both of us very nervous.

TOM:
What's that?

BIN:
How should I put it? We heard you are not making the payments on your new vehicle.

TOM:
Quite frankly, that's none of your business!

RICK:
In business, everything has to be transparent, Mr. Larvhaz!

TOM:
I still don't see what that has to do with you *two!*

BIN:
Well, sir, Mr. Vines and myself, well . . . we were practically threatened by a certain car dealer, if you know who I mean.

TOM:
(Furious) What? The Mercedes guy?

RICK:
You got it.

TOM:
What did he want?

BIN:
He wants his money, mister.

RICK:
Let me make this clear for you,
Mr. Larvhaz . . . We don't want to proceed
with the partnership any further. I appreciate your enthusiasm, but we are out of this
here deal!

BIN:
Yeah. We appreciate you, but . . . bye!

TOM:
You two are a pair of chicken—(Sputters) old
men!

RICK:
Mr. Larvhaz, we are not going to hear any
more of this nonsense. So do us a favor and
leave us to think about all this!

TOM:
After all the money I have invested in our
deal? Oh no! This will not end like this!
You'll hear from my lawyer!

BIN:
Sir . . . You do as it pleases you.

RICK:
Mr. Larvhaz, we would be happy to return your initial investment.

TOM:
(Confused) I only missed a few car payments . . .

RICK:
Tom, we don't want to hear no more! We are out!

TOM:
No! *I* am out! You'll be hearing from my lawyer!

BIN:
Go ahead. We have lawyers too!

(TOM walks away from the scene, while MATEO approaches RICK and BIN.)

MATEO:
What was all that noise?

RICK:
Mr. Naranja, nothing happened here.

BIN:
Oh, yeah. Everything's okay. What's *not* okay, is *this* boy. (Points at OSCAR)

MATEO:
Hasn't he finished, yet?

RICK:
No.

MATEO:
(To OSCAR) What are you waiting for, boy?

OSCAR:
Boss, this is a lot to process!

MATEO:
What I am going to process is the paperwork to fire you!

OSCAR:
You're firing me? But . . . why?

MATEO:
For being so slow—*that's* why.

RICK:
Even my four-year-old nephew Wyatt, would have finished *this* task by now.

BIN:
I agree with Mr. Vines, here . . . This boy has been working in slow motion.

MATEO:
You're embarrassing me, Oscar! Do you really want me to fire you?

OSCAR:
No sir! Please . . . I implore you!

MATEO:
Then . . . Finish *ASAP,* boy!

OSCAR:
(Monotone) Yes.

MATEO:
Yes, WHAT?

OSCAR:
Yes . . . sir.

MATEO:
Ah . . . Okay! I'll be back in a while.

BIN:
I hope that by then, this boy is done!

MATEO:
We'll see about that! (Walks toward his stand)

(TOM and SAVINA enter the tomato stand; both are hugging each other in a romantic way.)

TOM:
Baby, I am glad you came with me.

SAVINA:
Me too. Tom, you don't know how much you mean to me.

TOM:
(Smiles and turns away from SAVINA)
Well . . . By now . . . you know that I am a married man, don't you, babe?

SAVINA:
What's that supposed to mean, Tom? I love you.

TOM:
Savina, look. I care—I care for you. You know that, right?

SAVINA:
Care? That's it?

TOM:
Baby, (tenderly) this whole business depends on me. I can't mess things up!

SAVINA:
But . . . I don't get it! Why did you talk so sweetly to me, then?

TOM:
Look babe, it is what it is. What I feel for you is . . . kind of . . . sick. Trust me, you don't want to be involved with me.

SAVINA:
Then, why did you look for me? Why did you call? (Sobbing)

TOM:
(Laughing) I told you, babe. You don't want to be involved with me. I'm a bad boy.

(SAVINA walks away and sits in the central bench. OSCAR enters the scene and walks toward her.)

OSCAR:
Savina?

SAVINA:
(Sobbing) Oscar? Hi . . .

OSCAR:
Are you crying because of what Mr. Naranja did to you?

SAVINA:
What? Oh. no . . . it's not that.

OSCAR:
Then what is it?

SAVINA:
Tom Larvhaz.

OSCAR:
Tom Larvhaz? Oh, no. He's an animal, Savina. Stay away from him!

SAVINA:
Yes. Everyone seems to agree with you.

OSCAR:
Then . . . STOP! He is bad news, Savina.

SAVINA:
(Dries her eyes up) Enough about me. What about you? How are your wife and kids?

OSCAR:
Oh, they're great! You know my wife is also going to school, right?

SAVINA:
Yes, I see her on campus all the time.

OSCAR:
That's right. I forgot you also go to school.

SAVINA:
Thank God. I don't know what I would do if it wasn't for school . . . but . . . changing the subject . . . Are you still working for Mr. Naranja?

OSCAR:
Yes, I am. I heard what he did to you.

SAVINA:
Ah, that . . . yes, it sucks. He doesn't know how deeply that hurt my dad and me.

OSCAR:
Is there something I can do for y'all?

SAVINA:
Oh, no. Thank you, Oscar, but we'll be fine.

(Suddenly, MRS. LARVHAZ enters the scene while yelling.)

MRS. LARVHAZ:
Where is Tom? Where is that woman?

(RICK, BIN, and MATEO appear confused, while OSCAR and SAVINA appear frightened.)

OSCAR:
That woman. Savina, you must go! *Now!*

SAVINA:
Oh, boy . . . is she Tom's wife?

OSCAR:
I think so.

(MATEO walks towards Oscar and SAVINA.)

MATEO:
What do you think you are doing here? Wasting time, boy?

OSCAR:
I was . . . just talking to Savina.

MATEO:
You! (To SAVINA) Why are you taking time from my employee? Huh? You should leave, girl!

SAVINA:
But . . . I was just sitting here.

OSCAR:
Yes, we were just talking—that's all.

(MRS. LARVHAZ walks toward Oscar and SAVINA)

MRS. LARVHAZ:
Who is this woman?

MATEO:
Mrs. Larvhaz, I am Mateo Naranja.

MRS. LARVHAZ:
Ah . . . (Shortly) Nice to meet you, but who is this? (Points to SAVINA)

OSCAR:
She's my friend. Her name is Savina, ma'am.

MATEO:
But . . . wasn't she with Tom earlier?

OSCAR:
Boss! What the heck?

MATEO:
Well . . . she can tell Mrs. Larvhaz where Tom is, can't she?

MRS. LARVHAZ:
Were you with Tom earlier?

SAVINA:
Well, yes ma'am. I was.

OSCAR:
Savina, I think I'll take you to school, shall I?

SAVINA:
Sure.

(Both stand up from the bench and try to exit the scene)

MRS. LARVHAZ:
You two! Stop this instant!

OSCAR:
Why, ma'am?

MATEO:
Boy! How dare you talk to the lady like that?

MRS. LARVHAZ:
(She pauses to stare at SAVINA, her hand

over her mouth pensively, as if a realization is slowly dawning on her.) You! It *is* you! You're the woman my husband has in his cell phone! Come over here! (BIN and MATEO walk toward SAVINA, hold her arms, and try to force her to walk toward MRS. LARVHAZ)

SAVINA:
With all due respect, Mr. Naranja, you don't have any right to touch me! Neither do you, Mr. Cheapbarr!

MATEO:
God has given me the right to bring *justice* when sinners like you must be punished! Now walk, girl! Walk!

OSCAR:
But, boss . . .

SAVINA:
(Forcefully struggling) Let go of me, Mr. Naranja!

(After several efforts, OSCAR and SAVINA set themselves free and run toward backstage. BIN and MRS. LARVHAZ run after them)

MATEO:
STOP! THAT IS AN ORDER!

(Lights out)

THE BUSINESS PARK

Intermission

(The scene is decorated with balloons. There is a big banner that reads "Cheapbarr Annual Festival" hung between the tomato and the orange stands. TOM is with his wife, MRS. LARVHAZ, at his tomato stand, MATEO is with OSCAR at the orange stand. DAVE, BIN and RICK are at the counter bar; all are attending a number of customers.)

DAVE:
I am happier than a tornado in a trailer park!

BIN:
I heard that, Mayor!

RICK:
This shindig appears to be a success, folks!

BIN:
We need a serious talk with Mr. Mercedes.

RICK:
I don't have to talk about anything. Our lawyer will be handling that unfortunate situation.

(ANTHONY walks around while pushing the Frozen Iguana cart to sell ice cream.)

ANTHONY:
Ice cream! Ice cream! (Slight pause)

ATTENTION, PLEASE! (Everyone stops talking) We have a sponsor from Lake City, who has donated the great grand prize for this evening. So . . . y'all are welcome to Mr. Cheapbarr's stand to pick up tickets for the raffle!

(Everyone claps their hands. MARIONA enters with a big lunch box, approaching the counter bar.)

MARIONA:
Hello, there!

DAVE:
There she is! Welcome to the honky-tonk!

RICK:
What can we do for you, ma'am? Raffle tickets, perhaps?

MARIONA:
I was wondering if I could leave y'all some food boxes I prepared for the festival.

RICK:
What do you mean?

MARIONA:
Well, you can keep a commission for each box that is sold!

RICK:
Bin, do you know anything about *us* selling food boxes for Mrs. Goddard?

BIN:
Truth be told, no.

MARIONA:
Are we not good business buddies?

(Both men nod.)

MARIONA:
Well? I don't see a problem here. I'll tell you what, I'll be back in a few. How about that?

RICK:
No ma'am, with all due respect, since you're . . . well, a woman, I would suggest you go and find another venue for your merchandise.

BIN:
But Rick, it's no problem for us to sell those boxes, anyway.

RICK:
No, Bin!

MARIONA:
Bin, you always have sold the boxes for me at your festival!

RICK:
Ma'am, a lot of shady deals ended when Mr. Cheapbarr partnered with *me!*

MARIONA:
How *rude!*

RICK:
No ma'am, just fair and square.

MARIONA:
(To BIN) Are you going to remain quiet after what this jerk just said to *me*?

BIN:
Mrs. Goddard, Mr. Vines is my partner now.

(MARIONA rages then walks toward MATEO's stand. A few customers are shopping as OSCAR and LOUIS, the helper, stand while organizing jars of preserves.)

MATEO:
Howdy, Mrs. Goddard!

MARIONA:
Mr. Naranja!

MATEO:
Ma'am, how many times do I have to remind you to just call me Mateo?

MARIONA:
Okay, Mateo. As a matter of fact, Mateo . . .

MATEO:
There we go!

MARIONA:
I have a few lunch boxes I prepared with my own hands. Can I leave them here for you to sell for me?

MATEO:
For you ma'am, I'll reach the infinite and yonder.

OSCAR:
Boss, don't do it, please!

MATEO:
Boy, mind your own business!

OSCAR:
Sir, I already know the drill. It is *me* who is going to end up selling those boxes for this individual!

MARIONA:
Individual? Watch out, boy! You better learn to know your place!

OSCAR:
I refuse to sell food boxes for the very person who cost my friend Savina her account with Mr. Naranja!

MATEO:
Now you *did it,* boy! Apologize this instant!

OSCAR:
No! I will not.

MARIONA:
Are you going to let this simpleton treat me like that? Mateo, you are a businessman. Teach this boy his lesson!

MATEO:
Boy, if you don't apologize, you leave me no choice.

OSCAR:
What choice? Just say it Mr. Naranja . . . *say it!*

MATEO:
(Yelling) You are FIRED! Get out of *my* business.

OSCAR:
It would be my pleasure, sir. Ten years—*ten years* I've worked for you, and this is how you treat me? Savina delivered your meals, not a minute later than twelve noon for ten years. It didn't matter, rain or shine, she was always here for you, Mr. Naranja. How did you repay her?

(SAVINA approaches and interrupts OSCAR.)

SAVINA:
Oscar, no! Don't do this, you need this job.

OSCAR:
Mr. Naranja, why don't you tell everyone here how you paid Savina and her elderly father? Come on! Do it!

MARIONA:
Boy, you need to learn your place. You are completely out of order!

OSCAR:
You are the one who is out of place, ma'am! Why don't you sell your own lunch boxes, huh? Why don't you?

MATEO:
Boy, because she is a businesswoman! There are employees such as yourself who do that kind of job.

MARIONA:
That's right . . . Because I am a businesswoman. Actually, I'm heading to a very important wedding, and I don't have time for this, this time waster.

OSCAR:
(Removes his apron and hands it over to MARIONA.) Here. I'll pass this to you. I'm done wasting my time, ma'am. Let's get out of this nest of *rats,* Savina.

(Both walk away)

MARIONA:
I am speechless! Where did you find those inferior workers?

MATEO:
Mariona, I am appalled. I am speechless as well. I'll tell you what, hand over that apron.
(She hands it over.) I'll sell the boxes for you myself. How about that?

MARIONA:
Oh, that is so sweet of you. Thank you, Mateo. Now, if you excuse me, I have to leave.

MATEO:
Of course, of course. I'll have everything taken care of when you come back.

MARIONA:
Thank you, Mateo.

MATEO:
(To LOUIS, the helper) YOU! Take these lunch boxes and put them over there! (Points to an empty stand.)

LOUIS:
Yes, sir.

(TOM and his WIFE enter the scene and they walk toward the Cheapbarr counter.)

RICK:
Mr. Larvhaz, we don't want any mumbo jumbo going on here.

MRS. LARVHAZ:
Mr. Vines, Tom and I are fine. Aren't we, Tom?

TOM:
Oh, yes. We are just fine.

BIN:
I hope so. I just saw that Savina girl, down yonder . . .

MRS. LARVHAZ:
Mr. Cheapbarr, I don't have to worry about that meaningless woman.

BIN:
I am sure glad to hear that, ma'am.

TOM:
How is the tomato wine selling?

RICK:
Tom, like hotcakes on a platter! I'll tell you, I'd never have believed in such a thing.

BIN:
Yeah. We have sold almost all the crates you brought earlier!

TOM:
You see, gentlemen? It's good that we fixed our previous misunderstandings? Huh? (Both men nod.) I'll get more bottles, then.

BIN:
Keep them coming! Keep them coming . . .

TOM:
(To his WIFE) I'll be back in a jiffy, sugar! (Both kiss passionately, then he leaves the scene. ANTHONY enters the scene.)

ANTHONY:
Howdy, Mrs. Larvhaz. Do you have a raffle ticket?

MRS. LARVHAZ:
What is the prize?

ANTHONY:
Ah-hah! A big surprise from Lake City!

MRS. LARVHAZ:
Well . . . why not?

ANTHONY:
Here we go, ma'am. I'll give you five tickets—more chances to win. Ha-ha! (Walks away.) Tickets! Get your raffle tickets! All sponsored by The Frozen Iguana Ice Cream! Get your tickets!

(JESSIE enters the scene.)

MRS. LARVHAZ:
Jessie! Well—I mean . . . Mr. Mercedes.

JESSIE:
Well . . . if it ain't Mrs. Larvhaz herself! Outstanding, beautiful and delicate as an azalea blooming during springtime, in Macon County, Georgia.

MRS. LARVHAZ:
Oh, Jessie. I mean—Mr. Mercedes, you are too much! (Giggles.)

RICK:
If you come to talk about what we know, you better make yourself scarce, Mr. Mercedes.

JESSIE:
"What we know?" That matter has been clarified.

BIN:
Really? Like dust under the rug?

JESSIE:
Oh, better than that. Better than that, I'll tell you.

(JESSIE and MRS. LARVHAZ exchange looks)

RICK:
I sure hope so! Reckon, if that's over, let's get you something to drink! Ha-ha! *You!* (To HELPER 2) Bring the sensational, exquisite tomato wine for Mr. Mercedes and Mrs. Larvhaz.

HELPER 2:
Yes, sir.

MRS. LARVHAZ:
Oh, yes. Tom's wine.

(HELPER 2 brings the bottle.)

JESSIE:
(Abruptly grabs the bottle and reads.) Tom's wine. Wow! Ingenious! Tom's tomato wine. Good name!

BIN:
(Sets several wine glasses out and serves the wine to all.)
Let's make a toast: to the best deal of this year's Cheapbarr Festival, Tom's wine!

ALL:
Cheers!

(DAVE approaches.)

DAVE:
What about me?

RICK:
Mr. Montgomery. Just in time. Here! (Serves him a glass of wine.) Try this.

DAVE:
(Takes a sip) Whoa! This is good stuff! What is it?

BIN:
That, my dear Mayor, is tomato wine.

DAVE:
Are you pulling my leg?

RICK:
Nope! That's exactly what it is.

DAVE:
Yeehaw! Sweet and hot . . . spicy tomato wine!

MRS. LARVHAZ:
I made the recipe.

DAVE:
Did you?

MRS. LARVHAZ:
Yes, sir. I came up with the whole enchilada.

RICK:
This is the first time I heard of this, ma'am. Tom never mentioned anything.

MRS. LARVHAZ:
Mr. Vines, where in the whole world would Tom come up with the idea of mixing tomatoes with ginger, mejorana and the rest of the mystery ingredients in this concoction?

BIN:
I have to give you credit, ma'am.

RICK:
So, it was *you*, all along?

JESSIE:
(Approaches MRS. LARVHAZ closely.)
You're not only beautiful, but a little box of precious surprises . . .

MRS. LARVHAZ:
Thank you all!

BIN:
Well, let's keep digging in!

(All laugh.)

HELPER 2:
Can I try a little?

RICK:
Ha-ha! Don't be ridiculous, boy. (More customers approach the counter to buy more bottles.)
Go! And get back to your work, boy.

HELPER 2:
I just wanted to try. It's not a big deal.

RICK:
You want to try it? Then . . . work and *buy* it, son! That's how the world rolls.

HELPER 2:
Yes, sir. I guess you really know better.

MATEO:
What's happening here?

BIN:
We are celebrating! Come on over, Mr. Naranja. Come on and try Tom's wine!

RICK:
Yes. Tom's wine!

MATEO:
(Grabs a bottle and reads the label) Tom's tomato wine? Is that a thing?

BIN:
In your face! Ha-ha! Here! (Serves him a glass—MATEO has a sip.)

MATEO:
Whoa-whoa-whoa! Whoa . . . This is good stuff! *Wow.*

(TOM enters the scene while carrying a crate.)

TOM:
Howdy, howdy.

ALL:
(Start clapping, while singing.) Tom's wine! Tom's wine! Tom's wine!

MRS. LARVHAZ:
Babe, they love my wine!

TOM:
Your wine? What the heck? Are you out of your mind, woman?

JESSIE:
What's that supposed to mean? Mrs. Larvhaz gave you the recipe, didn't she?

(All stare at the LARVHAZ couple.)

MATEO:
(To LOUIS THE HELPER)
Hey *you!* Bring a few grapefruit preserves over here!

BIN:
But, why?

MATEO:
You guys owe me big time!

RICK:
Owe you? What are you grumbling about?

MATEO:
(Grabs a bottle and reads aloud the ingredients.) Spices, mejorana, bitter oranges! See? Bitter Oranges from Naranja Enterprises.

BIN:
Ah, I see. Sure, bring some preserves. After all, we all are businessmen.

(Everyone claps and laughs. ANTHONY enters the scene carrying a big cooler in his arms.)

ANTHONY:
The big prize has arrived! (Everyone claps.) Yeah, the big prize you all have expected! You'll no longer have to drive to see *one*, because you'll have it in the palm of your own hand! Do y'all want to see it? Come on, y'all hear me?

ALL:
(Everyone claps.) Let's see it!

ANTHONY:
Prepare to discover the gift that Lake City has to offer to the rest of all of us Floridians! Prepare, prepare!

(Puts down the cooler, opens it, and shows everyone.)

CUSTOMER 1:
It's a . . . baby alligator?

(BIN walks, stares at the cooler and nods sideways)

BIN:
Mr. Creamery, a gator? A Florida gator?

ANTHONY:
Exactly! A Florida gator. Florida is filled with gators. They identify us as Floridians! What better prize than that?

RICK:
Mr. Creamery, you never cease to surprise and amaze me with your innocent nonsense. Bravo! Bravo!

ANTHONY:
Well, thank you, Mr. Vines. So, who's ready to embrace this magnificent specimen? Are you ready to find out who is going to be the winner, huh?

(Everyone claps)

ANTHONY:
Okay. (Picks the bowl with tickets from the bar counter and draws a ticket.) And the winner of a Lake City baby alligator is . . . number 07081935.

MRS. LARVHAZ:
Oh, Gosh! I can't believe it! It's *me*! I have it! (Starts jumping with joy. TOM hugs her and she hugs JESSIE awkwardly, then walks toward ANTHONY.) Here! Here is my ticket.

(ANTHONY takes and checks it.)

ANTHONY:
Yes. I'm happy to announce Mrs. Larvhaz as the winner of the grand prize for this year's Cheapbarr Festival!

(Everyone claps.)

MRS. LARVHAZ:
Thank you. Oh gosh, I have never won anything. I am so excited, babe! (to TOM)

ANTHONY:
(Picks up the cooler and gives it to her.) Here is your very own baby alligator, Charlie!

(Everyone claps.)

TOM:
I'll tell you what babe, I'll take the cooler to our stand.

MRS. LARVHAZ:
Oh, you sweetie pie! Thank you.

(They kiss. TOM walks toward the tomato stand with the cooler while JESSIE approaches MRS. LARVHAZ.)

JESSIE:
Congrats, Mrs. Larvhaz!

MRS. LARVHAZ:
Oh, Jessie . . . this isn't the time or the place to talk about foolish things.

JESSIE:
So *now* you call it foolish? That's rich! After everything we went through together? You just disappeared into thin air.

MRS. LARVHAZ:
Keep your voice down. Someone might hear us.

JESSIE:
Why don't you tell your dear hubby the reason he still keeps his car? Huh?

MRS. LARVHAZ:
I think you should leave now!

JESSIE:
This is still a free country! Why didn't you tell me to leave when we were together?

(Grabs her arm, forcefully. TOM enters the scene.)

TOM:
What the heck is happening, here? Let go of my wife, Mercedes!

JESSIE:
Nothing is happening here, Tom.

TOM:
That's not what I saw happening!

MRS. LARVHAZ:
Tom, Mr. Mercedes is right. We were just talking.

TOM:
I hope so. Otherwise, I'll break his nose.

JESSIE:
Ha-ha. What if I dare you to do it anyway, huh?

TOM:
What did you just say, Mercedes? Repeat that!

MRS. LARVHAZ:
Enough you two! Enough!

(DAVE walks toward the three.)

DAVE:
Now . . . you three keep it down, keep it down. Have a good time instead, y'all.

MRS. LARVHAZ:
Of course, Mr. Montgomery, of course.

DAVE:
I'll tell you what! Tom, why don't you show me Charlie the gator, huh?

(TOM nods, and both men leave toward the tomato stand while MARIONA enters the scene and walks to MATEO's stand.)

MARIONA:
I am back, Mateo.

MATEO:
Howdy, there.

MARIONA:
How were the sales?

MATEO:
(To LOUIS, the helper) Hey, you! Did you sell the boxes I asked you to sell?

LOUIS:
Yes, sir.

MATEO:
Well, what are you waiting for? Hand the money over.

(LOUIS grabs the money from his apron and gives it to him.)

MATEO:
Here we go! (Hands the money to MARIONA)

MARIONA:
Thank you, Mateo! Just for that, I'll give you a big discount on your next lunch box.

MATEO:
Oh, that's mighty nice of you!

(JESSIE walks toward MATEO's stand and approaches MARIONA.)

MATEO:
Mr. Mercedes, what can I do for you?

JESSIE:
How is the business doing, Naranja?

MATEO:
Like a pearl coming out of a shiny oyster!

JESSIE:
Ha-ha! You're a funny man, Naranja. May I have a word with Mrs. Goddard, here?

MATEO:
Of course, of course! (Leaves)

JESSIE:
You sure have guts coming here, Mariona!

MARIONA:
What about you? Does Tom know about you messing around with his wife?

JESSIE:
The question is, does Mrs. Larvhaz know that *you* have been having an affair with her husband for years, now?

MARIONA:
What do you want, Jessie?

JESSIE:
You know? I actually don't want anything more than you keeping your pie hole shut. That's all.

MARIONA:
Is that a threat?

JESSIE:
Take it however you like.

(MARIONA leaves abruptly and heads to the central bench—SAVINA, LILI, OSCAR and PETRO, SAVINA's father, enter the scene.)

MARIONA:
(Starts clapping her hands.)
Ha-ha! Mateo's former employee has arrived, surrounded by a bunch of nobodies!

(When he sees SAVINA, TOM leaves his stand abruptly, accidentally leaving the cooler open, where Charlie the baby alligator is contained.)

TOM:
Savina, you came! (Hugs her) I am really glad you are here.

SAVINA:
Thank you.

PETRO:
Tom Larvhaz, long time no see! How's business?

TOM:
Great! I'm actually partnering with Mr. Cheapbarr and Mr. Vines.

PETRO:
Good, good. I am glad for you. Savi, I didn't know you had a friendly relation with Mr. Larvhaz. Why didn't you tell me?

SAVINA:
(Nervous) Well . . .

TOM:
I just gave her a ride home once. That's all.

PETRO:
Oh, well, thank you for looking out for my daughter. Savi should have called me, so I could pick her up! Oh, well.

(MARIONA approaches TOM)

MARIONA:
Tom! You don't say hello anymore?

TOM:
(Nervous) Mariona? I didn't realize you were here.

(LILI elbows SAVINA.)

LILI:
I think we're going to walk around to see more of the festival. Let's go, Savina!

(When SAVINA, LILI, OSCAR and PETRO are about to walk away, MRS. LARVHAZ walks toward TOM. When she sees SAVINA, she becomes furious.)

MRS. LARVHAZ:
You? How dare you show your face around here?

PETRO:
Ma'am, don't talk to my daughter like that. Have some respect!

MRS. LARVHAZ:
Oh, yeah? (To SAVINA) Why don't you tell your dad *why* my husband has *your* photo in his cell phone, huh?

PETRO:
Savina? What is the meaning of all this?

SAVINA:
I don't know why he has a picture of me dad, I promise!

PETRO:
Larvhaz? Why the heck do you have a picture of my daughter in your phone? Answer me!

TOM:
It was an accident, that's all; I swear, I thought it was my wife's photo.

MARIONA:
Ha-ha, I can't believe this! (Laughs) Tom Larvhaz involved with this insignificant individual? Is this how low you can get?

PETRO:
What I want to know is, who gave the right to the bimbos—*the entitled Karens*—of this town to treat my daughter like this?

MARIONA:
You listen to me, old fool!

PETRO:
Oh, no! No, no, and no! You listen to me lady, if I can even call a heartless individual who cost me a bunch of loyal clients a "lady." You have no idea the damage you have caused to my entire family, Mrs. Goddard.

MRS. LARVHAZ:
You are not going to swap the attention from your daughter to Mariona. Your daughter has messed around with *my* husband! What are you going to say about that, huh?

LILI:
You should be more clear as to who *really* messed with *whom*, ma'am. Let whoever is free from sin throw the first stone!

PETRO:
(To TOM) Larvhaz! Are you going to stand quietly by while these women fight all because of you? *You* are the one who should be speaking right now. After all, Larvhaz, you're the culprit in all this!

TOM:
Me? Why?

PETRO:
Tom, I knew your father. Actually, we grew up together. Did you know that? Your father and I used to run on the dirt roads of Loma

Linda, without shoes. He was one of the most honest, hard-working men I've ever met. God rest his soul. If he was alive, he would be ashamed of what you've done with his business and money. I already heard about the so-called "Tom's Tomato Wine." How dare you? I helped your dad pick tomatoes back in the day. Yes! We picked tomatoes for love of the priceless treasures earth provided us, and *you* have absolutely twisted all the principles your father based his company on. And on top of all that—you, my best buddy's own son, are trying to SEDUCE my daughter, who happens to be half your age! How dare you, Larvhaz? How dare you? Answer me!

TOM:
What I do with my wine is none of your business! Stay out of it. And with respect to your daughter, I didn't hold a gun to her head when she accepted my ride home.

MRS. LARVHAZ:
I want this girl to be held accountable. Why doesn't she speak? Talk! Explain. Why did you mess with my husband, who happens to be . . . a married man?

LILI:
Again, ma'am, you don't have the slightest right to even open your foul mouth.

PETRO:
Lili, please don't get involved in this, let them figure it out.

TOM:
(To LILI) No! I want to know what this young girl has to say. Why are you saying my wife should not open her mouth?

LILI:
That's a question you should be asking your wife, not me, sir.

TOM:
(To MRS. LARVHAZ) What is she talking about?

MRS. LARVAHZ:
Don't you see, dear? They are trying to . . . cloud the issue! You and this child (To SAVINA) should be addressing all *my* allegations. (Starts crying)

LILI:
Oh, really? Boo-hoo. *We*—in fact, everyone—in this town *knows*, ma'am.

MRS. LARVAHZ:
Knows what? Speak!

(JESSIE enters the scene)

JESSIE:
Yes, Lili, why don't you answer Mrs. Larvhaz's question?

TOM:
What the heck has all this got to do with you, Mercedes?

JESSIE:
Why don't you ask your wife, Larvhaz?

TOM:
(To his wife) What is he talking about?

MRS. LARVHAZ:
I don't really know. I swear to God.

LILI:
Oh really? (Laughs)

MARIONA:
I think Mrs. Larvhaz isn't telling the truth. Tell the truth!

MRS. LARVHAZ:
What are you doing here anyway? You don't have anything to do with all this.

LILI:
That's what you think, Mrs. Larvhaz!

MRS. LARVHAZ:
What's that supposed to mean? Are y'all trying to make me crazy, huh?

JESSIE:
Yes, Mrs. Larvhaz. Everything is

about *you*. Everything revolves around Mrs. Larvhaz and she never confronts any of the consequences.

TOM:
(Approaches JESSIE with a fist.) Now, Mercedes, I am going to punch you in the face. How dare you talk to my wife like that?

JESSIE:
DO IT! DO IT. Fight me like a man!

MRS. LARVHAZ:
(Takes her cell phone, dials.) I am calling 911. This has to stop!

LILI:
911? (Laughs) Just tell the truth and stop using cover-ups, ma'am.

TOM:
(To his wife) Speak, woman!

ALL:
Speak!

JESSIE:
Just say it! I want to hear the truth coming from your lips, or do you want me to say it for you? Huh?

TOM:
Say what, Mercedes? Say what?

LILI:
Say what? Oh (sarcastic) say what? Why does

Mrs. Goddard remain so quiet in the middle of this conundrum? There are also big juicy bugs coming from your own closet!

MARIONA:
You wench! Hush your filthy mouth!

LILI:
Oh no, no, no, no, no, no, no, no! You don't tell me what to do! Did you forget all you made me endure while I worked with you? The mighty Mrs. Goddard! Why don't you tell everyone here that you don't own the business you *say* you own? You are just an employee like the rest of the people there. I remember all the mistreatments and humiliations, the throwing under the bus, while you just gave in to all the wishes and commands of the *real* owner if you know what I mean.

MARIONA:
You are going to hush your foul mouth or . . .

LILI:
Or *what*? Huh? Or what? No, no, ma'am. This is not only about me and my former coworkers; this is about the hypocrisy of the elite. Ladies and gentleman, while this woman *of business,* the

mighty Mrs. Goddard appears in front of you all, all distinguished and all—she is a master of deceit. She takes what belongs to others without the minimum remorse, mercy or compassion. It's time she started paying for all she has taken from others! There must be justice in this world.

SAVINA:
Lili! It's not your place to make that happen. Please, stop. Please, I beg you.

MRS. LARVHAZ:
(To LILI) Why do you insist? Are you talking about Mariona? She doesn't have anything to do with Tom and me!

LILI:
Oh, really?

(MARIONA wags her head "no.")

(Suddenly, the entire crowd behind starts yelling.)

CROWD (VARIOUS):
Run! Look out! There it is!

(Behind the crowd, merchandise from TOM's stand falls to the floor while people run all over the place. There, in MATEO's stand, his merchandise also falls all over the floor. Everyone is hysterical and behaves like a crazy mob. ANTHONY enters the scene.)

ANTHONY:
Tom, Tom! Who left Charlie's cooler open?

TOM:
What?

ANTHONY:
(Hyperventilating) Yes! The cooler where Charlie the gator was stored?

MRS. LARVHAZ:
Who? What? Where?

ANTHONY:
Charlie is on the loose! He is crawling all over the place.

TOM:
Oh, no!

(TOM and MRS. LARVHAZ join the mob to catch the baby alligator.)

LILI:
Wow, Mariona. You were just saved by Charlie, the baby alligator. It appears that scum like you always get away with their wrongdoings.

MARIONA:
FOOL! The world belongs to the *smart* people, not to the *nice* people. Don't you ever forget it! Now if you are done with your foolishness, I have a business to run.

(Leaves the scene)

LILI:
YOU! YOU! (Abruptly, SAVINA grabs her hand.)

SAVINA:
Lili please, let her go. Let her go, Lili. Please.

PETRO:
Yes, Lili, let her go. There are people like her everywhere. Although we can't change the world, we can change little spots and dots to keep a certain balance. Now . . . Savi. What is all this about Larvhaz? Why am I just learning all this now?

LILI:
She just— (SAVINA interrupts her)

SAVINA:
Dad, I'm sorry. I actually . . . how would I put it? I fell for Tom.

PETRO:
WHAT? SAVINA . . . No!

SAVINA:
Yes, Dad. I fell for him terribly.

LILI:
Why do you think she has lost so much weight, Petro?

PETRO:
No! How could you, Savina? What's the matter with you?

SAVINA:
Dad . . . it's not what you think! I promise.

PETRO:
What do you want me to think?

SAVINA:
Tom made me feel worthy, beautiful, intelligent and more than anything else . . . desired. I never felt like that before. The first time I took a ride with him, I felt complete; like the luckiest girl in town. I couldn't snap myself out of the fact that those manly arms were maneuvering the steering wheel of the car I was riding. The chemistry between us was so strong that we could touch it; it was burning both of us at the same time. We started meeting for a cup of coffee at the Sterling's in Tavares. That stare . . .
the stare . . . We stared at each other, while his eyes sparkled like two little blue gemstones. I became a flirty young teenager; it became a game . . . a sweet game.

PETRO:
Is that why you started buying all those new dresses, shoes and makeup? (Cries)

SAVINA:
Yes, Dad. Yes . . . I felt beautiful . . . I was having coffee with the most beautiful man in town . . . one of the richest . . . what else can a girl ask for? And it was me . . . Savina . . . your daughter. I could not believe it. Just think about it, Dad, the more we met, the more I wanted him. I wanted to kiss him, touch him, I wanted to have him, Dad.

PETRO:
How dare you! Are those the principles I taught you? (Cries)

LILI:
Petro, let her explain. Let her explain, please.

PETRO:
I can't believe this—a *married* man! (Keeps crying)

SAVINA:
Yes, Dad, a married man. A married man who never wanted to touch me. I tried to touch him, Dad. But he always walked away from me. I wanted it all. I wanted *him,* but he pushed me away. Then he just vanished—vaporized—just like that. (Cries) He didn't call, didn't look for me, and ghosted my messages. The pain consumed me; it hurt so badly. Although we never touched each other,

I was so stupid to think that those coffee meetups meant that we were . . . actually dating. Desperately, I started showing up at his business place and he barely talked to me anymore; my heart broke into pieces. He said that he was a married man, that . . . (Cries)

LILI:
Petro . . . Larvhaz played with Savina's heart. It's very clear.

PETRO:
My dear child, why didn't you tell me anything?

SAVINA:
Dad, how could I? His dad was your best friend.

PETRO:
That doesn't mean anything! *You* mean everything to me. I hate to see you suffer for that dirtbag!

(Both cry and hug. LILI approaches OSCAR.)

LILI:
When are you going to make the big announcement?

OSCAR:
Soon . . . very soon. Just watch and see.

(Lights dim. A few moments of blackout transition before lights turn on the Cheapbarr counter bar. BIN, RICK, and MATEO are surrounded by FULL CAST, except for MARIONA.)

BIN:
Well, we wrap up this year's Cheapbarr Festival with domestic turmoil and the deranged baby alligator, Charlie, who destroyed our merchandise. Our dreams of a profitable event just went poof in front of our eyes.

MATEO:
But the Good Lord above is merciful and I know—I feel in my heart—He will provide. Yes, for each item we lost tonight, He will multiply them ten thousand times!

ALL:
Amen!

MATEO:
Hallelujah! God, have mercy.

(Everyone engages in some sort of collective prayer session. JUSTO FIDEL enters the scene.)

JUSTO:
(Ahem) Excuse me! May I have your attention, please?

(Everyone becomes quiet and stares at JUSTO.)

DAVE:
Have mercy! Well, if it ain't Justo Fidel. What brings you here?

JUSTO:
Mr. Montgomery, I am afraid I'm here to handle matters of business.

DAVE:
I don't get it. What does a former judge and college professor have to do with this business park?

(Starts laughing) Are we all in trouble with the law?

(Everyone starts laughing)

JUSTO:
Oh, no no. Even if you were in trouble with the law, my dear Mr. Montgomery, I no longer work for the federal justice system. I'm retired now, enjoying my horses down in Ocala and riding my hog on Sundays.

BIN:
So, why the heck are you here, Fidel?

RICK:
As far as we know, no one has called upon your services.

JUSTO:
Well, there . . . my friend . . . you are wrong.

BIN:
What the heck? Who called you, Fidel?

JUSTO:
A certain citizen whose life has changed dramatically in the last weeks.

MATEO:
(Rude) Who's that supposed to be?

JUSTO:
Ah . . . no more Hallelujahs, huh? No more Amens? As a matter of fact, my dealings here are linked to Naranja Enterprises, LLC.

MATEO:
What's that supposed to mean?

JUSTO:
Oh, yes, Mr. Naranja. I have an official notification addressed to none other than *you*. Here. (Approaches MATEO and gives him an envelope.) Would you be so kind as to open and read the notification out loud?

MATEO:
(He opens and reads the letter. His eyes become wider, his hands start shaking, and his mouth drops.) I'll be darned! Is this a joke, Fidel? Who gave you the right to do this? Are you crazy? Are you taking revenge, Fidel?

JUSTO:
For what? Ah . . . for the many times you needed my services and never paid? No, no.

MATEO:
I never paid you because you were a useless lawyer—that's why! That's why you retired!

JUSTO:
(Laughs) Mr. Naranja, you just admitted that you don't pay your debts. *Wow.* Regardless of whether the person is wrong or right, sir, if you incurred fees for legal proceedings, as a defendant, you are obligated to pay! But Naranja, you know well that those old debts don't have anything to do with the letter I just handed to you!

RICK:
So, what's the deal, then?

JUSTO:
Why doesn't Mr. Naranja disclose the contents of that letter?

MATEO:
I don't have to say a word here without my own lawyer.

JUSTO:
That's true. He's right this time.

MATEO:
I don't know what your game is Fidel, but just watch! (Tears the letter in pieces)

JUSTO:
Mr. Naranja, that doesn't even work in the movies. Listen, if you don't vacate your stand in the next two weeks, I have given the sheriff orders to take action.

MATEO:
How dare you? My stand? Everything I have worked for? *No!* Do you hear me? *No!* Who is behind all this? *Talk!* I order you, Fidel. *Talk!*

JUSTO:
Naranja, you don't order me. And I pray to God you never order anyone else for the rest of your existence.

MATEO:
Please, just tell me, who is behind all this? Please. (Cries)

(OSCAR, LILI, SAVINA and PETRO enter the scene)

OSCAR:
It was me, Mateo.

MATEO:
You? Biting the hand of the one who feeds you?

OSCAR:
The hand who FED me? Actually, Mateo, for ten years, I worked restlessly. The more I worked, the more I believed you

appreciated my labor. Sometimes I worked twenty hours in one single day—working long hours became my daily routine.

MATEO:
And this is how you repay me? Ungrateful piece of *trash!*

OSCAR:
What do you figure, in that over-sized-calculator head of yours, about all the money you made, while paying me less than minimum wage? Because, I actually have all the figures, Mateo.

MATEO:
So now I am just *Mateo?* No more Mr. Naranja, huh? No more boss? You scum. You are an illiterate ignorant. For God's sake, is this a joke? A prank, maybe?

LILI:
Did you say Oscar is illiterate and ignorant? *Wow!* (Looks at OSCAR) Didn't you tell this man that you were going to business school at night for all these years? What a lack of communication between employer and employee. I met Oscar while we were going to school together.

MATEO:
Business school? How could you?

OSCAR:
Actually, I mentioned it to you—repeatedly—but you never listened to anything I said anyway.

MATEO:
So now you want vengeance? Squeezing my sacrifice and efforts to steal them from me?

OSCAR:
Let me ask you, Mateo—didn't I ask you to *not* make your business public five years ago?

MATEO:
What?

OSCAR:
Yes, Mateo. Five years ago, you had the greatest year your business has ever had and you decided to put stocks for sale in the stock market.

MATEO:
Well, is that a crime? (Pauses) Wait a second . . . do you mean?

OSCAR:
I have been buying stocks from Naranja Enterprises, LLC for the last three years. Do you know why? Because I was the one picking up the oranges, the one who contacted the clients, the

one who came out with the new jelly recipes. It was me who listened to angry customers when they weren't happy with the merchandise. What were you doing? Clicking buttons on your calculator and computer. I knew I wasn't going to feed my wife and children with my pitiful income you provided me. So, I bought stocks of a business that I deeply loved and felt passionate about.

MATEO:
My business! Don't ever forget, *my* business, you thief!

OSCAR:
No, Mateo, I'm afraid you are wrong. Once you sell stocks of your business to the public, it is not *your* business anymore.

MATEO:
So, you want to evict me from my own business? Ungrateful pig!

OSCAR:
I wish, Mateo, but I am *not* like you. Although I bought all seventy-five percent of your shares, I'll keep just fifty and you can keep the remaining twenty-five percent.

JUSTO:
That's right. But there is a clause disclosed in the letter. Mateo, you are to leave the premises of this business park. As you all know, Naranja Enterprises, LLC has six other franchised stands throughout Florida. Mateo, you can choose three of those locations, except this business park.

MATEO:
So, I just became an employee with the snap of your fingers?

OSCAR:
Oh, no, Mateo. Again, I'm not like you. You will be an associate. I already distributed my fifty percent among Petro, Savina, my wife, and Lili. Actually, all of us are now associates.

MATEO:
What? Savina, too?

OSCAR:
Oh yes, Savina too. (Signals SAVINA to approach him.) She and Petro are now merging with us, and Lili will handle the administration.

MATEO:
(Talks to RICK, BIN, and TOM) Aren't any of you going to say something?

(They all wag their heads "no.")

JUSTO:
Mateo, there is another detail we haven't mentioned. This detail involves the businesses of Cheapbarr, Creamery, Vines and Larvhaz.

ALL FOUR MEN:
(They all act surprised) What is it?

OSCAR:
There *is* no Business Park anymore!
(Everyone reacts puzzled.)

JUSTO:
I am very pleased to announce that Oscar and his new partners have purchased this park.

BIN:
What the heck are you talking about, Fidel? We have been doing business in this park for decades.

JUSTO:
Well, Cheapbarr, this park is in the process of becoming an animal sanctuary. We've already made arrangements with the city, and the park is going back to the *people* and *animals* of this community.

TOM:
I know what this is all about.
(Approaches SAVINA furiously) It's *you*,

isn't it? This is how you are taking revenge against me? What about *you,* Petro? My father was your best friend, did you forget about that? Huh?

PETRO:
Did you remember my friendship with your father when you decided to play with my daughter? And God only knows how many girls fell for your sweet talking. All of you—the so-called *businessmen* of this park—remained here for years without paying rent thanks to the mayor, here! (Points to DAVE) The everlasting mayor of this city!

DAVE:
Well, as members of the chamber of commerce, they were exempt.

JUSTO:
For God's sake, Mr. Montgomery. We all know what happened at this park. Years ago, these businessmen decided to trespass on this park, and open their business against the will of the people. Did you care, then? *No!* Meanwhile, Mr. Montgomery received substantial contributions from you all for his never-ending reelections.

DAVE:
I am going to sue you for defamation.

JUSTO:
Defamation, my rear end! I have seen all the legal documents. For God's sake, you know better than that, Dave. (Laughs and points to the businessmen) You are all very wealthy older men, why haven't you spent all this time enjoying your grandchildren? Your retirement?

OSCAR:
I know why, Justo. Control. This business park is in a very strategic spot where they can control the trade of their products.

BIN:
Since when is it a crime to be a businessman in this country? We businessmen can't be nice all the time; that's not what business is about, and you should know that by now.

OSCAR:
Bin, to be a businessman isn't a crime, but to run a business rent-free, knowingly *is*.

RICK:
That's not our fault. The opportunity presented itself, and we took it.

OSCAR:
Let me ask you, Rick, how much have you

given back to the park? But more importantly, how well did you treat the people of this community? The employees?

BIN:
We gave y'all work. We gave you a way to make a living, and this is how you'll pay us?

OSCAR:
Bin . . . Let me ask you, what's my name?

BIN:
I beg your pardon?

OSCAR:
Yes, what's my name?

BIN:
Why the heck would I have to know your name, huh?

OSCAR:
Wow. For ten years, you've borrowed me from Mateo to do your chores.

BIN:
Oh, Billy! That's it. Your name is Billy . . . I plumb reckon.

RICK:
No, Bin. It's *Oscar*. His name is Oscar, and he's right. (Pensive) We should be enjoying our family, traveling,

enjoying the ice cream of the Frozen Iguana on Daytona Beach—not here, Bin. Think about it, didn't you miss your own son's wedding at one point? Huh? The birth of our grandchildren, their chorus recitals, dance performances, baseball and football games, theatrical shows, our children's weddings . . . even (scoffs) funerals—for *what*, Bin?

MATEO:
(Clapping his hands) So, now you turn against the rest of us, huh? You *rat!*

RICK:
Yes Mateo, I guess I *am* a rat. I have ratted my own loving and faithful family. I feel ashamed of myself.

(Turns face down)

BIN:
Rick, is that the way you really feel? Well, it isn't the way *I* feel.

ANTHONY:
What *do* you feel then, Bin?

BIN:
I feel . . . (He pauses) I feel fear. Fear of being alone, or not having anything to do. I'm scared of not having money to face the future. I'm fearful of being forced to live in a nursing home. *Fear* of losing . . . losing . . .

ANTHONY:
The control, perhaps?

(BIN nods—RICK puts one of his hands on BIN'S shoulder.)

TOM:
You two can say all this rubbish, because you are old. But I'm still young and don't intend to give in to what Oscar and Savina want to do to me.

SAVINA:
Oh, it's always about *you*. Isn't it, Tom? This is about justice and fairness. It isn't about you. All of us know you don't need to be in this business park. You're a well-off man. Why do you insist on remaining somewhere you don't belong? This place doesn't belong to you either.

ANTHONY:
Savina, he wants to remain here because if he loses this place, he loses control of whatever this sanctuary means to him.

PETRO:
Is that true, Tom? I know perfectly well about the fortune you inherited from your dad. (Chuckles) I actually helped him to amass such a fortune. He was always good and clever for business, and I wasn't. Tom . . . (Approaches him) you

don't need this. If you simply love making money and business deals, just for the thrill it gives you, you can do it anywhere else. Let it go, please.

TOM:
(To SAVINA) I never meant to hurt you, Savina. You, of all people. You have got to believe me, please.

(TOM and SAVINA exchange reflective glances while silence prevails for few seconds.)

MATEO:
RATS! This isn't going to end like this. Oscar, you and the rest of all *you rats* will hear from my lawyer!

JUSTO:
Then you and your lawyer will hear from me. How about that, huh?

(Furiously, MATEO leaves the scene. Tom turns and gives Savina one last longing glance, then follows Mateo offstage.)

OSCAR:
Anthony!

ANTHONY:
Yes, sir?

OSCAR:
Why don't you sell us some ice cream from the Frozen Iguana Cart?

(Everybody celebrates.)

ANTHONY:
Well, that is going to be a little difficult.

BIN:
Why is that?

ANTHONY:
Because I am not carrying ice cream in my cart today, it's . . . something else, instead.

RICK:
Oh, Mr. Creamery, are you playing with us? Come on, open the Frozen Iguana. It's hot enough to fry an egg on the sidewalk.

(Everyone starts fanning their hands.)

ANTHONY:
No, seriously. I'm not carrying ice cream today.

PETRO:
Ah, let me see! (ANTHONY tries to stop him and lifts the lid of the cart and looks surprised.) Well, if it ain't none other than Charlie!

(Everybody starts running around like headless chickens.)

ANTHONY:
Wait . . . where did everybody go?

(OSCAR, SAVINA, PETRO, LILI, BIN, RICK, and ANTHONY circle around the Frozen Iguana cart, looking at CHARLIE the gator.)

OSCAR:
Actually, Anthony, it was a good idea to not carry your ice cream today.

ANTHONY:
Oh, really? Why is that?

OSCAR:
It gives us the opportunity to introduce the first official inhabitant of the business park to his new home.

ANTHONY:
Who? Charlie?

OSCAR:
You got it, my friend. Please, Anthony, do us the honor of tilting the cart so Charlie can walk free.

ANTHONY:
That would be an honor, sir.

(String puppet of the alligator is pulled from backstage to make it look as if he is crawling toward the woods.)

BIN:
Wait, wait . . . this occasion deserves a toast. Come over to my counter.

(All walk toward the counter and BIN starts distributing wine glasses among the group, pouring the wine.)

RICK:
Oscar, why don't you do us the honor of naming the occasion for this toast?

OSCAR:
If you insist, Mr. Vines! (All lift their glasses.) Today marks the day of a new beginning. Some of us will decide what is the next chapter of our lives, while others will face what is next upon their horizons. They'll do so with feelings of joy and enthusiasm for all challenges that lay ahead.

ANTHONY:
A toast for my sweet comrade Charlie. He found his freedom today.

PETRO:
And with freedom, this business park is officially open. I toast to that!

SAVINA:
Open for business! Cheers to the business of bringing people together.

LILI:
For the business of protecting the defenseless. Salud!

OSCAR:
Today, for the first time, this business park is open for business. Salud!

ALL:
Salud!

(All freeze lifting their hands while holding their wine glasses. Lights down.)

THE END

About the Author

Albalis Vargas-Smith, a.k.a. Lirio Blanco Show, is an architect, painter, muralist, and writer from Panama. She received her undergraduate and graduate degrees in architecture from Universidad Autonoma de Centroamerica in San Jose, Costa Rica. In addition, she received a bachelor's degree in fine arts at Auburn University, Montgomery. She has more than twenty years of experience in architecture, having worked both in Montgomery, Alabama, and the Atlanta area. She has done theatrical scene and set design as volunteer work for community theatre groups.

Back in July 2016, Albalis went solo as an entrepreneur architect, founding the Vargas-Smith Studio. The reason? To spend more time with her daughter. In 2020, she decided to finish a series of backburner short stories and theatrical plays, which are presented in this book.

Currently, Albalis lives in Johns Creek, Georgia, with her daughter, husband, her dog, Toni, and their precious bird.

www.ingramcontent.com/pod-product-compliance
Lightning Source LLC
Chambersburg PA
CBHW030551080526
44585CB00012B/338